Illustrated Review
of
Ottumwa, Iowa

1890

PBL Limited
Ottumwa, Iowa

This edition copyright 2011 by PBL Limited
Cover and design copyright 2011 by Michael W. Lemberger

Originally published in 1890 under the title *Descriptive Illustrated Review of Ottumwa, Iowa,* by Fred. G. Flower, assisted by Claxton Wilstach

This edition published 2011. Type has been reset and photographs enlarged and restored from the original.

10　9　8　7　6　5　4　3　2　1

ISBN　1-892689-90-1
ISBN 13:　978-1-892689-90-0

Photo credits: Photographs and illustrations are reproduced from the original edition of *Illustrated Review* unless otherwise noted here. The following illustrations are from the collection of Michael W. Lemberger, used with permission: Front cover and title page - Union Depot. Page 43 - Father Francis Ward portrait. Page 78 - Myer C. Rice Clothiers. Page 93 - Federal Building under construction. Page 123 - Thomas Dove Foster portrait. The following illustrations are from the Longdo collection, used with permission: Page 59 - The Fair. Page 95 - Hall Candy Company.

Original copy of *Illustrated Review* provided by Mike Crowder.

Printed in the United States of America

All rights reserved. Except for brief passages quoted in any review, the reproduction or utilization of this work in whole or in part, in any form or by any electronic, mechanical, or other means, now known or hereinafter invented, including xerography, photocopying and recording, or in any information storage and retrieval system, is forbidden without the express permission of the publisher. For permission contact:
　　Rights Editor
　　PBL Limited
　　P.O. Box 935
　　Ottumwa IA 52501-0935
　　pbl@pbllimited.com

Copies of this book are available from PBL Limited. Visit our website at www.pbllimited.com for more information.

...DESCRIPTIVE...

ILLUSTRATED REVIEW.

— OF —

OTTUMWA, IOWA.

TRADE, COMMERCE AND MANUFACTURES.

EDITED AND COMPILED BY
FRED. G. FLOWER, Assisted by Clarton Wilstack.
1890

Title page from the original 1890 edition

Ottumwa 1890

Ottumwa - 1890
View from the tower of the Coal Palace,
looking almost directly north over downtown and residential areas

2011 edition

Preface to the 2011 edition

Many things have changed about the city and about the language in the 120 years since this book was first published. In 1890, the current courthouse did not yet exist, the public library occupied "two rooms in a central location", and the most commanding structure in the city was the brand-new Coal Palace.

Since that time, some streets have been renamed, and the numbering system for city addresses was updated. Street addresses listed in the book, though accurate at the time, may not be reliable on today's maps. For example, in 1890, Green Street continued south across the river into South Ottumwa, and south side streets were not yet numbered, or divided into north and south. House numbers and locations for the homes pictured in the book are from the 1890 Ottumwa City Directory.

Things have also changed in society. Only a few women are mentioned in the book, and even fewer are referred to as business people or entrepreneurs.

Readers will note several features about the book which seem odd or even unacceptable today. Many phrases have changed in 120 years, but – for example – in 1890 secretaries used *type-writers* and took *short-hand*, and *to-day* generally contained a hyphen. *Per cent.* was two words and included a period because it was (and still is, for that matter) an abbreviation of *per centum*. *Colored* was an acceptable term of reference for non-Caucasians.

Alphabetizing and abbreviations are erratic, and spelling varies from one reference to another. Occasionally a name is spelled one way in the text but differently in the caption. We have maintained spelling, paragraphing, and inconsistent references as produced in the original, in the spirit of accurately reproducing the information in the book.

However, the text has all been reset for added clarity. Today's technology has also allowed us to place photographs directly alongside the related stories, rather than grouping them together on separate, special plates as in the original. Most of the photographs are reproduced in a larger size than in the original book.

We wish to thank Mike Crowder, who loaned his original copy of *Illustrated Review of Ottumwa, Iowa* to assist in this republishing effort.

Michael W. Lemberger & Leigh Michaels, editors

Ottumwa 1890

...PREFACE....

THIS book is compiled and published for general distribution. Each and every citizen of Ottumwa is interested in the distribution of the work, and to accomplish the object aimed at, it is to be hoped that copies of it will reach every English-speaking country in the world. Those who receive copies will have friends to whom they will want copies sent, and in this way the whole edition will find its way to the people whose best interests it will serve.

The price of the work is $1.00. Those desiring extra copies will find them on sale at the store of the leading newsdealer of this city—J. T. Perdue, 223 East Main Street. Parties desiring copies sent by mail must enclose ten cents with which to pay postage.

F. G. F.

Preface to the 1890 edition

2011 edition

The State of Iowa

Iowa reminds one of the witty and clever small man who was made the butt of mild ridicule at a banquet table by the other guests, all of whom happened to be men of splendid stature, because of his diminutive form. One gentleman was so pointed in his remarks that the small man felt called upon to defend himself, and, rising in his seat, he called the roll of great men, dead and living, who were noted for their small forms, not forgetting Stephen A. Douglas, Napoleon Bonaparte and others, ending his defense of "little fellows" by an impromptu rhyme, as follows:

"Were I so tall I could reach the sky,
 Or grasp the ocean in my span,
'T would be the same to you and I—
 The mind is but the stature of the man."

This forceful truism is applicable to states and territories, and to none is it more thoroughly applicable than to the State of Iowa. In area ranking twenty-second, yet in many products ranking first in quantity and quality among the great manufacturing, grain, stock and mineral-producing states of the Union.

The report of the Agricultural department for the year 1888 (the latest report obtainable at this writing) contains the following table showing Iowa products and their values:

PRODUCT.	AMOUNT.	VALUE.
Corn, bushels	321,269,962	$73,974,891
Wheat "	19,814,000	15,744,340
Oats "	78,681,814	15,342,953
Rye "	1,954,924	781,956
Barley "	3,815,424	1,507,087
Buckwheat, bushels	336,000	245,280
Potatoes, Irish and Sweet, bushels	19,929,924	5,134,716
Grass Seeds, bushels	785,000	1,151,100
Flax Seed "	2,265,750	2,514,982
Hay, Timothy, tons	5,077,800	25,235,175
Hay, Prairie "	2,000,000	7,680,000
Broom Corn "	3,200	230,858
Sorghum, gallons	2,297,629	1,083,929
Horses, number	1,033,022	74,632,082
Mules "	45,649	3,996,540
Cattle and Oxen, number	2,095,253	42,638,398
Milch Cows, number	1,255,432	29,251,565
Hogs "	4,148,811	27,969,624
Sheep "	408,478	884,430
Products, orchard and vine		2,500,000
Products, hive		500,000
Products, poultry		5,000,000
Products, dairy		15,000,000
Products, small fruits		500,000
Products, timber		3,000,000
Miscellaneous products, other than above		10,000,000
Total		$365,179,917

Ottumwa 1890

The $10,000,000 credited to miscellaneous products covers the coal mined and sold that year. These figures speak plainer and have more force than would volumes of general statements from an unofficial source. The foregoing table was incorporated in the report of the Hon. Frank D. Jackson, secretary of state, and to whom we are indebted for much valuable information. The same report gives the number of miles of railroads in the state at 8,298 with an assessed valuation of $43,271,008. The school statistics show 15,611 ungraded schools in the state, giving employment to 25,793 teachers, 5,432 of whom are males. The enumeration of scholars in 1888 showed a grand total of 649,606, of which number 489,229 were enrolled in the public schools. The number of school houses is placed at 12,879, with a total value of $12,580,345. What an eloquent tribute to the intelligence and patriotism of an advanced civilization these figures prove. No state in the union boasts of more schools or better, more churches or better, than Iowa. The influence of these institutions is forcibly proven by the marked decrease of criminals in the state as shown by the secretary of state's report. In 1883 the total number of convictions in all the courts, for all crimes, was 1,377, while in 1888 it was but 838. During this time the number of legal voters increased from 327,283 to 404,130. So much for the schools and churches. We will now mention some of the state institutions which are aiding in making the social atmosphere of Iowa what it is. In their alphabetical order they are as follows:

Agricultural College,
Agricultural Society,
Board of Dental Examiners,
Board of Health,
College for the Blind,
Commissioners of Pharmacy,
Educational Board of Examiners,
Historical Society,
Horticultural Society,
Hospitals for Insane, three,
Improved Stock Breeders' Association,
Industrial Schools, two,
Institution for Deaf and Dumb,
Institution for Feeble-minded,
Penitentiary, two (only 260 inmates in both),
Soldiers' Home,

2011 edition

Soldiers' Orphans' Home,
State Normal School.
State University.

These give further proof of our claim that the State of Iowa is abreast of every other in the maintenance of all public and private institutions which aid the advancement and education of her people. Many other claims for recognition could be made, many other reasons given why it is the best state in the West for the thousands of emigrants annually leaving the East to settle in, but we will only mention one or two more, first of which is a climate of no extremes (in southern Iowa) and a mortality rate low as the lowest. The Assistant Secretary of the State Board of Health, Mr. F. L. Andrews, sends us a comprehensive statement on the subject, from which we quote as follows: " * * * records have not been tabulated since 1887, but *this we know,* that in 1880, with a population of 1,624,616, the death rate was 16 per 1,000 of the living population. In that year the State Board begun [sic] its work. In 1885 the population was 1,849,913, an increase of 225,299; yet, through the sanitary and preventative measures of the State Board, the death rate was reduced to 4.5 per 1,000, and that is very near the rate in 1889. Few, if any, states have a lower mortality rate." Next in importance is our splendid railway facilities and the great home markets for the majority of all products of the soil and mines; then we have splendid public highways, great water-power systems, beautiful rivers, lovely scenery and best of all an enlightened cultured people, proud of what their state has achieved, of her great resources and bright prospects for still greater achievements. Land is cheap, the soil rich and very productive, climate mild and agreeable and all conditions favorable to the happiness and comfort of all who seek and find a home among us. Many states and localities are making strong bids for a portion of the great army of people who are annually leaving the rocks and clay soil of the Eastern States in search of more fertile, productive land, with better markets and more favorable conditions. The claims made for some portions of the West and South, if true, would leave Iowa with a mighty poor show for securing any of that army of these home- seekers. No wild claims are made for this state, and such statements and figures as we have presented are to be relied upon as absolutely true in every particular, and we simply ask those expecting to change their place of residence to give Iowa careful consideration and comparison with all other states and we will be satisfied with the verdict. Come and see what a happy, prosperous, contented people we are, and you will become one of us.

Ottumwa 1890

Ottumwa

HER HISTORY, GROWTH AND RESOURCES. — A COMPREHENSIVE REVIEW OF THE PRIDE OF IOWA.

The illustrations in this book speak more for Ottumwa, its beautiful streets, handsome residences, substantial business blocks, towering mills and factories, grand churches and school buildings, and lovely scenery than anything its editor could possibly say. These cuts were made from photographs taken by a skilled artist under the direct supervision of the editor and are correct representations of the subjects presented. They are but a moiety of what could be published, but they truthfully mirror the many others of like kind and character.

Ottumwa is located, principally, upon the low hills which line the north shore of the Des Moines river at this point. There is sufficient level ground between the river bank and the first rise in elevation for the business and manufacturing interests of a city many times its size. Here are to be found her great mills and factories and her business streets, while between them and the river are located the large yards of the C. B. & Q., the C. R. I. & P., Wabash Western, C. M. & St. P. and the Iowa Central roads. The hills are not abrupt and precipitous, the rise is gradual and forms locations for residence purposes unsurpassed by any in the state, overlooking as it does the beautiful, rich valley of the Des Moines river. The city was platted to conform with the direction of the river, and in consequence thereof the streets run southeast and northwest and northeast and southwest. The drainage is the most perfect imaginable and results in healthfulness far in excess of that enjoyed by any city of like size within the boundaries of the state. The climate is equable and the air bracing and pure. The winters are short and mild, the summers cool and enjoyable. The city's magnificent churches and school houses speak volumes for the people's intelligence and are the very best criterion of what her society is. So much for Ottumwa as a place of residence, but, grand and stately as are her dwellings, beautiful as are her green lawns, noble shade trees, handsome streets, glorious climate and lovely scenery, they are secondary in importance to the great natural advantages to be considered by the merchant and manufacturer seeking a new location. If the reader will take a map of the United States, the fact will be very apparent that Iowa is in the very center of a world of consumers of every product under the sun – an empire containing from ten million to fifteen million souls. This being true, why shall not Iowa furnish these people with nearly every article of necessity, if not luxury, consumed by them. And why shall not Ottumwa lead all other cities of the west in manufactures? She has one of the finest water powers in the state, and enjoys the further and still greater advantage of being in the very center of one of the greatest fields of bituminous coal lying between the Atlantic and Pacific oceans, and of a quality excelled by none. This coal is placed at the door of the mills and factories at from fifty cents to one dollar and one dollar and a quarter per ton. Five lines of railways pass through or have their terminus here, and a

View from the tower of the Coal Palace, showing the Union Depot in the foreground, with the Market Street and Jefferson Street Bridges over the Des Moines River.

Ottumwa 1890

sixth one is in course of construction, the Santa Fe, giving to the city as advantageous facilities for transportation as any city in the Union. Freight rates are low, and, with the increased competition of a new road, promise to be still lower. We have many mills and factories, but we want many more; there is room for them, they are needed, and splendid remuneration will reward those who early take advantage of present conditions and remove their machinery or goods to this Lowell of the West and begin operations.

Here we have a combination of conditions and circumstances which can not be ignored by any one, and more especially the merchant and manufacturer seeking a change of location, and to each and all of them we extend a warm invitation to come and investigate our claims; see our busy mills, filled with well-paid, contented workmen; our grand business structures, stocked with goods from all parts of the world; our handsome streets, our noble schools and churches, the cozy homes of the laboring classes; see contentment and happiness on all sides; a charmed circle, as it were, of happy, thrifty people, from which grim-visaged poverty has been long excluded. Ottumwa is entitled

Union Passenger Depot (remodeled in 1950, the building is still in use as a depot)

View from the tower of the Coal Palace, showing the busy railroad lines
leading to and from Union Depot.
Five railroad lines served Ottumwa in 1890.

to the name of Lowell of the West, her factories and mills are many, but best of all, no Eastern money-lenders have mortgages upon her resources, either public or private; and in this respect she most resembles her namesake, Lowell, Mass. Further on in the book we will speak of the schools, churches, civic societies, public improvements, water power, the beautiful Coal Palace and many other matters of interest. To give the reader a clear and definite idea of all the different business interests of the city, we have thought best to write short sketches about some of the mills, factories and business houses and their founders or proprietors. This is done without their solicitation and without compensation, the cost of the entire work being met by popular subscription.

Ottumwa 1890

THE COAL PALACE.

    The crowning achievement of the enterprising people of Ottumwa is their beautiful Coal Palace. Space will not permit of the detailed description of its splendor and magnitude to which it is entitled. An exhaustive history of the great structure from its inception to the present, would make a good sized volume of itself, therefore, we must confine ourselves to the presentation of the principal features of interest. The idea of a Palace was concieved [sic] by Col. P. G. Ballingall, one of Ottumwa's oldest, most highly respected and enterprising citizens. The undertaking was not received kindly by the people, when first presented for their consideration, because of their lack of experience in such matters, and a lack of confidence in its accomplishment of the aims and object sought — advertising the city's and surrounding territory's resources. Many public meetings were held, subscription books were opened, and everything possible done to awaken public interest in the scheme. Col. Ballingall, Messrs. Manning, Flagler, Meek and others, were leaders in the work of securing subscriptions, and right royally did they apply themselves to the task. For nearly two years these men labored to secure the $30,000 necessary to insure the completion of the structure, and to them more than all others, is due the credit of giving to the world the first and only coal palace ever erected. The structure was completed and the finishing touches given to the interior decorations, September 15, twelve hours previous to its being opened to the public. The first day was made a gala day in the city and all citizens took part in the opening exercises, thronging the great building from early morning till late in the night. From September 16 to October 11, the doors of the Palace were open to visitors, and during the entire period, there was not a day which did not bring a crowd within its walls varying from two thousand to twenty thousand people.

    The dimensions of the Palace from one extreme to the other are, in round numbers, two hundred and thirty by one hundred and thirty feet. The main tower is two hundred feet high. The first story is twenty feet between the ceilings, and the second story about sixty feet. The main entrance is on Main street, directly beneath the great tower. The design of the structure is novel and decidedly original, being a compromise between the gothic and Byzantine, as a glance at the picture on the first page of the book will show. The interior

2011 edition

The nation's only Coal Palace, built in 1890 and located near Union Depot, was open for two seasons (1890 and 1891).

decorations were something so strikingly original and yet harmonious and artistic, that no effort will be made by the editor to describe them in the manner they deserve. Corn, oats, hay, wheat, rye, wool, hemp, coal, etc., were woven, so to speak, into all manner of designs, pictures, pyramids, etc., producing a most pleasing effect. The cost of the interior decorations was ten thousand dollars, not to mention the great number of valuable articles contributed by the ladies of the city, and the many days spent by them assisting in the work. There were exhibits made by ten counties, of the products of their mines, farms and mills, these counties comprising nearly all the coal territory in Iowa, and all being adjacent to Ottumwa. In their rank as producers of coal they are as follows: Mahaska, Keokuk, Wapello, Lucas, Monroe, Marion, Appanoose, Jefferson, Davis and Van Buren. Aside from the displays made by these counties were a number from other portions of the state, and many very striking and expensive exhibits by local merchants, factories and mills. Each one of the foregoing counties had a day set apart for them, and each showed their deep interest in the Palace by sending many train loads of people to the city on the days set aside for them. The first day Gov.

Ottumwa 1890

Boies was present and delivered the opening address, which was listened to by six thousand people. Col. Ballingall, president of the palace association, started the machinery of the building at the conclusion of the governor's speech, the large flag on the tower was hoisted, all the bells and steam whistles in the city took the cue, and for the next half hour conversation in all parts of the town was at a standstill—the coal palace was opened. The Iowa State band was present the entire first week. The second day Ex-Gov. Crittenden, Mo., was present together with Gov. Boies. The third day was Railroad day, being devoted exclusively to the reception and entertainment of railway men and officials of Iowa roads. Fourth day belonged to Van Buren county, and was notable for the size of the delegation from that rich county. Wapello county (of which Ottumwa is the county seat) claimed the fifth day, and it was celebrated by an attendance far in excess of any previous days. The sixth day was not set apart for any one county or locality. The Pella Band, known as the "Gilmore Band of the West," arrived for the week. The seventh was the "Red Letter" day of the Palace, Barnum's circus being in the city. It was Lucas county day, and an immense crowd came down from that county. It was estimated that thirty thousand strangers were in the town, twenty thousand of whom visited the palace. Following this came Miners' day, and from the hundreds of mines in the state came train loads of miners. They paraded the streets, and at the palace were addressed by State Labor Commissioner Sovereign. Eighth was Monroe county day. Five thousand people were present and in the evening they witnessed the opera "Powhattan," presented by local talent. The next and tenth day was Burlington and Missouri day, when, by request, the opera given the previous evening was repeated to a crowd which filled the great structure. It will be well to here mention the fact that Ottumwa boasts of a large number of ladies and gentlemen possessed of marked talent as actors and actresses, as their work in the rendition of "Powhattan" amply demonstrated. The eleventh day was a memorable one, it was set aside for the Traveling men. The people considered discretion the better part of valor and surrendered to the attacking forces early in the day. The Mayor of the city told the "boys" that the people wished to surrender unconditionally and to prove that it was not a scheme to draw the "grip soldiers" into ambush, they were presented with the keys to the city. Everybody here will remember that day. The twelfth day was for the Cedar Rapids people and they responded by sending a number of train loads of culture and refinement. Marion county, with its population of thirty thousand people, came down and claimed the thirteenth day. They sent a very large delegation. Knights of Pythias Knights of Labor and Des Moines people touched elbows on the fourteenth day, and one of the finest parades of the season was made by their combined forces. October 2, the fifteenth day, was Woodmens and Jefferson county day. A very large crowd was present. Blue Grass and Davis county were given the same day, and it was celebrated by the presentation of the opera, "Mikado," in the evening to an immense throng, the cast of characters being nearly the same as in "Powhattan." Ladies' day, October 4, was a great day for the fair sex. They came from all portions of the state. They enjoyed an exceptionally fine literary and musical programme and undoubtedly got more real pleasure out of the trip than any previous or subsequent delegation. The seventeenth day was down for Base Ball day, but was changed to the Saturday following. The Bloomfield band was in attendance. Keokuk day came next, and this thriving city sent five long excursion loads of people. Rev. Smalley, of Chicago, lectured in the evening, his subject being, "A Dream of the Twentieth Century." Next came Soldier's day, which was devoted to the greeting and entertainment of the old battle-scarred veterans. The nineteenth day was called Mahaska county day, but it proved to be everybody's day. President Harrison was the guest of the coal palace city, and, it being the first time that a real live president of the United States had ever stopped in Iowa, it was made the occasion for one of the largest demonstrations ever indulged by any city in the state. A conservative estimate of the number of people who greeted the President, places it at sixty-five thousand. It is needless to go into details regarding the reception tendered the president as it did not differ materially from those given him in other large cities. He was right royally entertained by the leaders of wealth and fashion in Ottumwa, and he went away feeling that no more hospitable, cultured people exist than are to be found among the fifteen thousand comprising our city's population. Mrs. T. J. Devin, for many years a resident of Ottumwa, is a sister of the President and all of his spare time, during his fifteen hours' stay, was spent with her in the quiet of her comfortable home. A pleasing incident during his stay was the presentation to him of a copy of the Ottumwa *Daily Courier*, printed upon silk, by its president and publisher, Mr. A. W. Lee, which the President acknowledged in a neat little speech, concluding with the remark that he would keep it as a memento of one of the most pleasant and enjoyable times spent on his entire journey. The twenty-first day was Appanoose county day, and it was by no means the smallest in point of numbers, there being three or four thousand people who were unable to get into the Palace the day previous, and who remained in the city over night for the purpose of visiting it. The last day, Oct. 11, was Base Ball day, and during the entire day and

Ottumwa 1890

1. P. G. Ballingall, President.
2. Dr. W. B. Smith, Director.
3. S. A. Flagler, Vice-President.
4. Calvin Manning, Secretary.
5. J. C. Manchester, Director.
6. Henry Phillips, Director.
7. A. W. Johnson, Director.
8. W. T. Fenton, Treasurer.

Directors of the Ottumwa Coal Palace

evening the building was crowded with people from far and near. The following Monday the school children, and all the poor people of the city, were admitted free. It is needlees [sic] to add that the Palace was a thorough success, financially, artistically and morally. It was a great undertaking and the people of the city are deserving of unstinted praise. Besides adding to the prestige of their beautiful city they have thoroughly advertised its manifold advantages, they have added a chapter to history's pages, they have covered themselves with glory —they built the first Palace of coal.

The present officers of the Coal Palace Association are as follows: President, Col. P. G. Ballingall; vice-president, Samuel Flagler; secretary, Calvin Manning; treasurer, W. T. Fenton. Directors: J. W. Garner, Henry Phillips, J. E. Hawkins, W. T. Harper, Geo. Withall, Dr. W. B. Smith, J. G. Meek, A. W. Johnson, J. C. Manchester.

BLACK DIAMONDS.

The last official figures showing the coal out-put of all coal producing counties in the state, places it at 3,864,490 tons. These figures are for 1887, and are compiled almost exclusively from the records of mines shipping by rail, no account being taken of the many hundreds of mines confining themselves to local trade – delivering their coal by wagon to the nearest towns, and to consumers in the immediate vicinity. The out-put of these mines if accounted for, would swell the figures to over 4,000,000 tons for 1887. The output for 1890 is estimated to be nearly 6,000,000 tons. The coal producing counties of the state are as follows: Adams, Appanoose, Boone, Dallas, Davis, Greene, Guthrie, Hamilton, Hardin, Jasper, Jefferson, Keokuk, Lucas, Mahaska, Marion, Marshall, Monroe, Muscatine, Page, Polk, Scott, Story, Taylor, Van Buren, Wapello, Warren, Wayne and Webster. Mahaska county leads with 895,548 tons; Keokuk, second, with 599,007 tons; Wapello county, fifth, with 272,073 tons. The coal, of this, like that of all other counties of the state, is bituminous, is the equal of any mined in the United States, and falls but six per cent. below the anthracite coal of Pennsylvania for practical purposes. The analysis, as shown by the report of Prof. White in his Geological Reports is as follows: Volatile combustion, 42.92; Fixed carbon, 49.70; Ash, 7.38; Total combustible, 92.62; Coke, 57.08. Consumption: Carbon, 87.25; Ash, 12.75. These figures are the average for the state. There are some counties producing coal showing 95.27 per cent. carbon with but 4.73 per cent. ash. As these are official figures, it seems unnecessary to dwell longer upon the coal deposits and their values. There are twenty-eight counties in the state producing coal which finds a market in Wisconsin, Minnesota, Dakota, Nebraska, Missouri, Kansas, Utah, Idaho, Wyoming, Montana and even in Illinois, one of the most prolific producers of soft coal. The amount of capital invested in this industry it is impossible to determine, but it is many millions of dollars, and gives employment to many thousands of men at excellent wages. The benefits to the people of the state from the coal industry is second only to that of agriculture.

Ottumwa 1890

Allen Johnston home - 531 N. Court

REAL ESTATE.

There never has been anything resembling a boom in real estate in Ottumwa. This fact is decidedly in its favor, and will materially aid in bringing outside capital here for investment. There can be no possible doubt about investments in city and suburban property proving exceptionally remunerative. Ottumwa is on the eve of a building and manufacturing boom which must, of necessity, send real estate upwards. And even if this were not true, the natural growth of the city, judging by the record of the past, would make an investment here one of the safest and best paying possible to find. Property in the business center of the city ranges from one hundred to one hundred and fifty dollars per front foot, this being for the choicest locations. Residence lots can be bought for from one hundred to five hundred dollars per lot, the latter price securing one of the choicest. All residence lots have a frontage of forty feet or more, and all are one hundred and thirty-two feet deep. Titles to all lands in this county are perfect, there being no cloud upon any portion of them, being deeded from the government to original settlers and purchasers – it is a well known fact that Iowa land titles are the best in the country.

Fred W. Wilson home - 420 E. Fourth

E. E. McElroy home - corner Wilmer & Chester Avenues

BUILDING.

The present year has witnessed the erection of more new buildings than any previous year in the history of the city. It is impossible to secure a correct record of the number, but it will not fall far short of two hundred, the cost of which will exceed one million dollars. A large number of fine business blocks have been erected and more are planned to be built in the spring of 1891. A glance at the cuts in these pages will show the reader the class of business and residence structures which adorn our streets.

Ottumwa Opera House, located at the northwest corner of Main and Jefferson, was barely completed when this photo was taken for the *Illustrated Review*

Ottumwa 1890

RAILROADS.

Ottumwa has five great railway lines reaching to or passing through her limits. No city of the West is better supplied with shipping facilities. The C. B. &. Q., east to Chicago, and west to all points in Iowa, Nebraska, Colorado and Wyoming; the C. M. & St. P., east to Chicago and Wisconsin points, north to Dakota and Minnesota, and west to Iowa, Nebraska, Wyoming, Colorado and Montana; the Wabash, south to St. Louis and all intermediate points, including nearly every prominent city in Missouri, and north to many principal cities of Iowa; the C. R. I. &. P., reaching all principal points in Illinois, Missouri, Minnesota, Dakota, Nebraska, Kansas, Colorado and Indian Territory; the Iowa Central, reaching all principal points in Iowa. The Santa Fe road is soon to build into the city, thus adding to the prestige of Ottumwa as a railway center and opening up a new territory reaching south to the Mexican border. According to her needs, this city has railway facilities equal to Chicago, and freight rates are equally as low. Manufacturers and merchants find no cause for complaint against discrimination or excessive charges. Iowa has rigid railway laws and the people have thus far looked to it that they were enforced.

DIRECTORY.

Attention is called to the directory among the back pages of this book, where may be found the names of such business firms, factories, mills, etc., as do not appear in other parts of the work. Together they form the only complete business directory ever published in Ottumwa.

BUILDING MATERIAL.

Splendid six to eight-room cottages are constructed here at a cost of from three to eight hundred dollars. Brick bring from six to eight dollars per thousand delivered; stock brick from ten to twelve dollars per thousand. Building stone is very cheap, there being vast deposits of it, and of the very finest quality. Dimension lumber brings from fifteen to twenty dollars per thousand feet, and flooring from seventeen to thirty dollars. Plaster is twenty cents per yard. When it is remembered that excellent lots, 40 feet front, can be bought for from one hundred to five hundred dollars per lot, and houses can be built for the above figures, it is no cause for wonder that nearly every mechanic and laboring man here owns his own home.

Post office building, completed in 1889. This building was replaced in 1910 by a new federal building on the same site, which is now Ottumwa's City Hall.

Ottumwa 1890

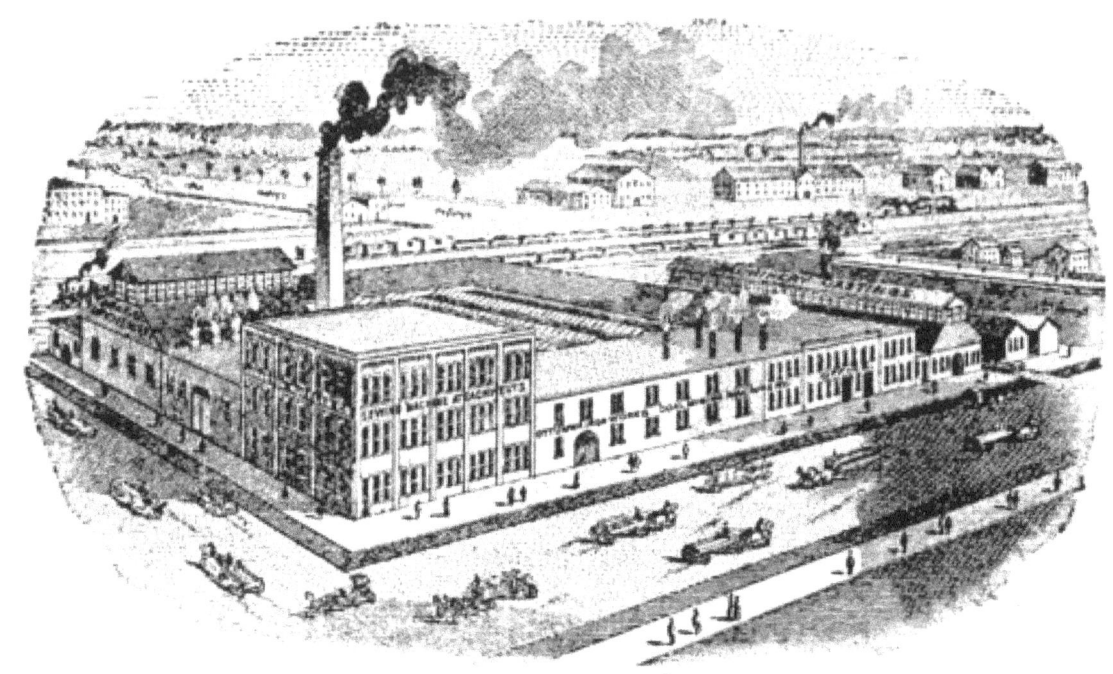

JOHNSTON RUFFLER CO.'S WORKS.

MILLS AND FACTORIES.

Ottumwa has many large mills and factories, notably among them being the following: Johnston Ruffler Co.; manufacturing sewing machine parts, mill machinery, etc.; Union Iron Works, Western Machine Works, drill factory, starch mills, linseed oil mills, pork packing house, two flouring mills, one stave factory, three barrel factories, one hardwood sawmill, four planing mills, one cigar box factory, four sash, door and blind factories, two screen door and sash factories, one woolen mill, one chair factory, two box factories, three brick mills and yards, one cutlery factory, one bridge manufactory, pickle factory, two boiler shops, three wagon and carriage factories, one plow factory, tombstone manufactory, one paper box factory.

2011 edition

Ottumwa Starch Works - foot of Wapello Street

Linseed Oil Mills - located at the corner of Cass and Samantha

Ottumwa 1890

Though called the Second Street Baptist Church in the *Illustrated Review*, this church was actually built on West Third Street in 1875. It later became the YWCA and then the Knights of Columbus Hall, and was destroyed by fire in 1982. The tower in the background belongs to the First Presbyterian Church located at Fourth and Washington.

CHURCHES.

Ottumwa has eighteen churches, very many of them being handsome, expensive structures, which would do justice to any city in the country. Their lofty spires are discernible to people living many miles away. Some of them are conspicuous for their massive proportions and others for their beauty of design, symmetry, harmony of colors, finish, etc. Probably no city in the Union of fifteen thousand inhabitants can boast of so many and fine churches, all in the most prosperous condition. Cuts showing many of these noble structures appear elsewhere in the book, they speak louder than words of the high standard of morality and intelligence of the people. Tell me the number of churches in your town and I will tell you whether I wish to become one of its citizens or not. This is a question which should first reach the lips of the man who contemplates removing to a city of which he has but little or no previous knowledge. This is but one of the many commendable features which makes of Ottumwa a most desirable place of residence.

2011 edition

Fourth Street Methodist Church (now First Methodist) at Market and Fourth.

South Side (Second) Congregational Church, located on the southwest corner of Division and Davis

South Side (South Ottumwa) Methodist Church, located at Willard and Church. This building burned and was replaced by another on the same site.

St. Mary of the Visitation Catholic Church, Fourth and Court. Replaced by a church constructed on the same site in 1930.

Ottumwa 1890

Main Street Methodist Church, built in 1874, located on the northwest corner of Main and College

St. Patrick's Catholic Church (called the South Side Catholic Church in the *Illustrated Review*), located at Church and Ward. This building was replaced in 1956 by a new building on the same site.

Congregational Church, built in 1874 on Fourth Street between Market & Green, next to St. Mary's Episcopal Church

2011 edition

St. Mary's Episcopal Church, northeast corner of Fourth and Market, built in 1865. The building was later a Christian Science Church after the Episcopal congregation constructed a new building at Fifth and Market. The site is now a commercial development.

This building was the third home of the First Presbyterian Church, located on the northeast corner of Fourth and Washington. Dedicated in 1889, it served the congregation for more than 25 years. Now the site of an office building.

Ottumwa 1890

Hedrick School, West Second Street

Garfield School, corner Ash and Plum

SCHOOLS.

The people of Ottumwa are proud of their public schools. There are six large brick structures of which any city would be proud, as reference to the cuts on another page will prove. The cost of these buildings was about $200,000. The number of pupils enrolled the present year exceeds 2,400. Sixty teachers are employed. To show that Iowa is in the van in educational matters we will give the State school statistics for 1888. No. of schools,

Lincoln School, Court Street between Washington and Marion
(Replaced in the 1950s by another Lincoln school, built on the same site, which later became Ottumwa Christian School)

Adams School, College Street between Second and Fourth.
Adams School was moved in about 1920 to allow space to build the high school.

15,611; No. of teachers, 25,793; No. of scholars, 649,606; average cost of tuition per month, $1.79; total value of school buildings, $12,580,345; total disbursments [sic] for salaries, etc., for 1889, $6,848,128.

South Side School, Church & Richmond --the first school building in South Ottumwa. Later known as Irving School, it was torn down in the 1970s and is now the site of McDonalds at Five Corners.

Ottumwa 1890

Y.M.C.A.

The Young Men's Christian Association of Ottumwa is a potent factor in assisting to maintain the high standard of morality for which the young men of this city are conspicuous at home and abroad. The association is in a healthy condition, having at present two hundred members. A new building is now in process of erection on the corner of Second and Washington streets, which, when completed, will be one of the handsomest, most substantial and best equipped Y. M. C. A. buildings in the West. The basement will contain bath rooms, bowling alley, gymnasium, barber shop and lockers. The first floor is being fitted for business rooms, while the second floor will contain the working rooms of the association, viz.: reception room, parlor, library rooms, reading room, secretary's public and private office, boys' room, class rooms, lavatory, cloak and check room, and an audience hall divided by rolling partitions for special occasions. The third floor will be occupied by a local business college. The building complete will cost $35,000. The officers of the association are: W. E. Chambers, president; A. D. Moss, vice-president; M. B. Hutchinson, treasurer; Irving S. Watson, general secretary. Much praise is due Mr. Watson for his untiring efforts in the work of securing subscriptions for the new building.

NEWSPAPERS.

The city is well supplied with excellent newspapers, both daily and weekly. The *Daily Courier* is an eight-page evening paper, which would do justice to a town of many times the population of Ottumwa. It is ably edited and always filled with telegraphic and local news. It is the only paper in the city receiving Associated Press dispatches. It is controlled by a stock company of which A.W. Lee is president. The *Daily Democrat* is a morning paper, devoted to the interests of the Democratic party and local affairs. It is an eight-page sheet, bright, newsy and well printed. It is edited and published by R. H. Moore. There are seven weekly papers, six English and one German, as follows: *Weekly Courier, Weekly Democrat, Weekly Press, Sun, World, South Ottumwa News* and *Weekly Freie Presse* [sic]. The *Courier* is the oldest paper in the county, having been published since August, 1848.

BLUE COATS.

The police service of the city is excellent. There are ten men on the force. They have no difficulty whatever in preserving order. Few arrests are made for serious offenses. The people are peace loving and quiet. This department appears to be a luxury, kept up to add to the metropolitan appearance of the city. Mr. Daniel Hannon is chief of this department, having held the position for ten consecutive years. E. F. Johnson is deputy marshal.

First National Bank Building, Market & Main. Replaced by a new bank in the 1920s.

PUBLIC LIBRARY.

The city has a library which would do credit to a place many times the size of Ottumwa. It now contains six thousand volumes, all handsomely bound and in excellent condition. Historical, biographical and classical works predominate, and their well-thumbed pages give ample proof of being often read, and also evidencing the intelligence of the people who patronize the library. The association occupies two very large rooms in a central location. Miss V. E. Sanford is librarian, having held the position for twelve years. T. H. Eaton, the popular cashier of the Iowa National Bank, is its president.

Ottumwa 1890

SOCIETY.

The common definition of this term is a "set," a chosen few of the wealthiest and most highly educated(?) [sic], who lead in introducing the latest styles in dress, who know all the latest fads of fashion's world, who entertain, give parties, go North in summer and South in winter, who know how to say something nice at the proper time and when to refrain from saying anything, how to be exclusive, how to appear English, in fact who know what is proper at any and all times. Well, Ottumwa doesn't happen to have an organized "set," but it has hundreds of families who know how to entertain, who have palatial homes where every comfort aud luxury known to the people of the Nineteenth Century may be found. They do not require an exhibition of one's bank account before their doors are opened. They are educated people, very many of them being graduates of Yale, Harvard, Princeton, Cornell, Vassar and other noted colleges; they are, as a rule, people who have spent much time in traveling over this and foreign counties; in a word, they are a refined, generous, progressive people, whom it is a pleasure to meet, but taken as a whole they are not what a society woman would call society people.

W. T. Harper home
1008 N. Court

Samuel Lilburn & Co. buildings - 226 - 228 E. Second & S. Green

FIRE DEPARTMENT.

 The service in this department is exceptionally good and especially so in the manufacturing and business portions of the city. The Holly System is used. Five hose carts are located at intervals of a few blocks through the business portion of the city with ample hose for any emergency. The department has one engine but it is not often called into use as disastrous fires, with one exception, are something not recorded in the history of the city. The efficiency of this department under the management of the present chief, Mr. J. D. Stevens, is cause for universal comment and praise. There are nine men in the service, a few of whom are termed volunteers—engaged in other pursuits. The officers of the company are: J. D. Stevens, chief; C. A. Calhoun, foreman; W. Rogers, secretary; John Corneilson, treasurer; Jim Judkins, assistant foreman. Mr. Judkins has been on the force twelve years and during that time has never been two blocks away from the central station on foot, has never had an accident befall him or his hose cart, and has had but one leave of absence during the entire period.

P. G. BALLINGALL.

To P. G. Ballingall, more than any other one man, is the growth and prosperity of Ottumwa due. No man stands higher in the confidence and respect of the people of the city and state. No man is more loved for nobility of character. No man is more often appealed to for assistance. No man is possessed of more charity and brotherly love. No man gives more or works harder for the welfare of the city, and no man can accomplish greater results. He is pre-eminently the first citizen of Ottumwa. A prominent newspaper of the state, in speaking of him, closes a brief biographical sketch as follows : "The citizens of Ottumwa are beginning to learn that they have a man in their midst who is worth his weight in gold—and if all would follow his aspirations, Ottumwa would almost become the center of the universe. He is an omniprescent [sic] and almost omnipotent spirit. His business is everywhere, and he turns his hand to everything. The press is wild in his praise, and those who envy him his position must yet learn to pay him homage." That these words of praise are fully merited by Mr. Ballingall, every man, woman and child of Ottumwa knows—it is not fulsome praise. To give a complete biographical sketch of his life would occupy more space than can be given to one man in these pages. He is of Scotch parentage, and is fifty-nine years of age. He is as active to-day, physically and mentally, as he was thirty years ago. He has been a hotel keeper nearly all his life. He built and owns the Ballingall House here. He has been president of the Iowa Hotel Keepers' Association and vice-president of the National Hotel Keepers' Association, from each of which he has received valuable testimonials. He has headed the Iowa delegation in the last three democratic national conventions, and has represented this district in the last two legislatures, first as assemblyman and next as senator. He was chosen as World's Fair Commissioner, but declined. As elsewhere stated, he is the father of the Coal Palace, and to him, primarily, its erection is due. He has risen from major to major-general of the state militia, and of which he is also the father. For eighteen years he represented his ward in the city council. He is president of the Wapello County Agricultural Society, and president of the Coal Palace Association.

CALVIN MANNING.

Calvin Manning, for many years city attorney and now the legal advisor of the Iowa National Bank, is one of Ottumwa's most highly respected and popular attorneys and business men. He is a graduate of Cornell University and of the Iowa Law University. Everybody knows Cal. Manning and everybody likes him. In public affairs he always takes a deep interest and an active part. He is secretary of the Coal Palace Association, and no man worked harder or more persistently than he for its success—it is safe to say it would not exist but for his great efforts in its behalf.

OUR ILLUSTRATIONS.

F. L. Briggs.

The cuts appearing in this work are so exceptionally fine that we feel it our duty to mention the photographer and engravers, as to them alone is their superiority due. Mr. F. L. Briggs, of this city, made most of the photographs. That he is an artist can readily be understood by a casual glance at the cuts. They are clear and strong, excellent in perspective, full of character, strength of detail and purity of tone. No photographer is capable of turning out finer work. It is not too much to say that Mr. Briggs should seek a wider field, for he is certainly capable of holding his own with any artists in this country. Geo. W. Thomas and J. M. Winn, well known photographers of the city, are entitled to the credit of furnishing some of the excellent portraits for the work. Vandercook & Co., 407 to 425 Dearborn street, Chicago, are the engravers. That they are not excelled by any in Chicago or the East will be evident to any one who will interest themselves sufficiently to compare their work with that of other firms. Great credit is also due Messrs Donohue & Henneberry, the printers (and binders), for the clearness and beauty of the cuts, as it is a well-known fact that the best of cuts can not make good pictures unless in the hands of experienced printers possessed of superior facilities for doing the work. This firm employs six hundred skilled workmen, and they are capable of turning out work the equal of any from the leading houses of this country or Europe.

Ottumwa 1890

RESUME.

Ottumwa is decidedly metropolitan. She has fifteen thousand inhabitants, about three thousand of them skilled mechanics engaged in the mills and factories.

She has five great railway lines, and a sixth one coming, a splendid electric railway system ; eighteen beautiful church edifices; six massive school buildings, a splendid steam supply system; a water power unsurpassed in the West; largest jobbing houses in Iowa; cheaper fuel than any other city of equal commercial importance; unexcelled transportation facilities, freight rates low as the lowest; is in the very center of one of the greatest coal districts in the world; is surrounded by the richest farming and mineral-producing districts west of Ohio, and the most densely-populated ; has a jobbing trade of over $4,000,000 annually; has expended over one million dollars in new buildings and public improvements this year; is possessed of a manufacturing trade of over $6,000,000; has a banking capital of $500,000, and deposits of $1,000,000; her homes and business buildings are free from mortgages; her bonded indebtedness is only $71,000 ; her taxes average but seventeen mills on the dollar; she conducts the largest and most successful fair in the state outside the State Fair; her streets, public buildings, and a majority of residences, are lighted by electricity; one mile of brick pavement was laid this year, which will be followed by four or five miles additional in 1891; she is the only city which successfully furnishes fuel gas; she has beautiful streets, hundreds of handsome residences ; beautiful scenery ; a lovely climate, healthy and invigorating; educated, progressive citizens and the first and only coal palace in the world. No city can offer greater inducements for investment or for the location of mills and factories.

COME AND SEE US.
R.S.V.P.

SOUTH OTTUMWA.

It is the privilege of the writer to pen the first historical sketch of the fifth ward of the city — known as South Ottumwa — having earned this distinctive title not only on account of its location on the south side of Des Moines river, separating it from Ottumwa proper, but by virtue of its individual struggles for growth and development and the wonderful enterprise it has always evinced. In 1857, when the Western fever was running high, a syndicate was formed in Albion, N. Y., for the purpose of investing in and developing some Western town site. It consisted of Sanford E. Church, ex-governor, of New York; Noah Davis, Judge of the Superior Court of New York; Chas. H. Moore, Afford Raymond and R. S. Smith. Having been elected prospector for the company, R. S. Smith started westward to choose a site. Arriving at Clinton, Ia., he found three others on the same errand, and together, having purchased a span of horses and a "democrat" wagon, they moved westward. After prospecting six months in Iowa, Mr. Smith selected the two hundred acres which are now part of South Ottumwa, and purchased them of D. P. Inskeep. At that time the only appearance of a town was a settlement of four or five buildings at the river bank, called after Dickens' jolly but erratic hero—Pickwick— named by the owner, the late J. L. Dickson, who was an ardent admirer of the great English novelist. The five members of the syndicate in the East each owned an equal share in the enterprise, but Mr. Raymond, weakening, sold his share to R. S. Smith, who, in 1858 moved to Ann Arbor, Mich., with his family. He died in 1876 without realizing whatever golden dreams he may have had of the success of his Iowa town site. It became the lot of his son, Dr. W. B. Smith, to continue the development of South Ottumwa, and how well he has carried out his father's plans is the household talk of its inhabitants, in testimony of which stands a beautiful little city of 2,500 population, where fourteen years ago there were only empty and unsold lots. The trials and vicissitudes of its early promoters were charaterized by the same hardships and opposition that marks the advancement of most new towns. Finding the old wooden toll-bridge which stood just east of the present iron structure a detriment to closer communication with Ottumwa, they succeeded in having a new free bridge voted by the county—not, however, until defeated in two elections. Even then the stockholders of the toll-bridge influenced the commissioners to delay the

Ottumwa 1890

Dr. W. B. Smith

building for two years until, as Dr. Smith sys: "The Lord, being on my side, a flood carried off the old bridge and they had to build in 1880." Then Dr. Smith laid out streets and built sidewalks at his own expense, helped people build homes, and a roseate dawn of prosperity burst upon the new settlement. Lots were donated to churches, and the Catholic, Congregational, Baptist and Methodist edifices, shown by illustrations, were soon erected in succession named. Dr. Smith expresses himself largely indebted to the Rev. Father Francis J. Ward for assistance rendered at this time in building his fine church and residence. Dr. Smith let the school district have nine of his finest lots for which he had been offered $2,500 in consideration of $800, and upon condition that they build a good brick school of two stories and not less than eight rooms. This splendid building, which cost $18,000, is shown in an illustration.

In 1886, South Ottumwa was annexed to the city. A year before, having about thirty *bona-fide* residents, the south-siders were organizing a village corporation, and had it about completed, when the city council met and passed a resolution extending the city limits so as to encompass this little town in its boundaries. A city vote carried this, and Dr. Smith served papers enjoining the measure. The case was lost to him in the circuit court, and upon being called by appeal in the superior court, it was found that records held by the Recorder had taken wings and flown! Acknowledging his defeat, unfair as were the means, Dr. Smith paid $50 attorney's fees and gave up the case, and returned to attack from another point. As South Ottumwa was joined to a ward across the river, and was paying out taxes from which it derived no benefit, the next movement was to make it an independent and individual ward. Bitter opposition was met, but, after a hard fight, with the aid of his friend, Hon. P. B. Ballingall, then a councilman, Dr. Smith carried his point and secured a representation of two aldermen in the council.

One of the most stirring epochs was the event of laying the street railway. A charter was applied for in 1884, which, instead of being granted to the south-side applicants, was given to parties whose object was to oppose the development of that side, and who kept the franchise for two years without making any effort to build. Finally Dr. Smith financially aided R. T. Shea to secure the franchise and the road was built under the following exciting circumstances. On a Saturday in the spring of 1886, previous to the Monday on which the charter was to expire, there had to be a great deal of dodging around to escape an injunction instigated by the enemies of the smith side. That night the cars bearing the rails, ties and street cars, all purchased outside of the state, which the railroad company, by virtue of a smart fee, had held awaiting orders several miles from town, were quickly drawn in and unloaded at the south end of the railroad bridge. Women and children turned out at midnight to lend aid by holding lanterns, and every boy and man able to work, fell in with a will. At 5 A. M. this novel undertaking was completed; all the while the opposition element lay unsuspectingly asleep, awaking to find the mule cars standing at the corner of Main and Market streets in the city of Ottumwa to give them a ride over the two miles of this "mushroom" railway. All of that Sunday crowds rode over this nocturnal curiosity, and the opposition were so exasperated that they formed in a body to tear up the tracks. The south-siders stood ready to defend their rights, and trouble was only averted by the sheriff dispersing the belligerents. Dr. Smith was to receive one-third interest in the enterprise as a recompense for his aid and money, but the agreement was violated and he lost his money, although he considers himself well paid from benefits the city has derived.

Real estate did not bring very fancy prices at first, lots 66 x 132 being sold for $75, that now bring $500 to $600. In the last ten months they have built over 200 houses, averaging $1,500 apiece, and the number of large brick store buildings has surpassed all previous years. Next year there will be 300 buildings erected without any doubt. Water mains have just been lain [sic] and many hydrants have been set in place. Electric light illuminates the streets, stores and residences. Several merchants have transferred their business to this side and more are preparing to follow. The most conservative estimate the population of South Ottumwa one year from now at 4,000. A division station of the Chicago, Ft. Madison & Des Moines railroad is a probable acquisition. South Ottumwa has the following thriving industries: Ainley's complete roller process flour mill, Wagner Bros. & Slavin's planing mill and feed mill, Lindsay's Apairist supply factory and bracket works, Sponsler's screen factory, A. S. Cook's cigar box factory, Hartman's wagon shop, Dan Chapman's saw mill, Russell's Shaw steam laundry, Stark Brothers' cigar factory, Underwood's tile works, and other smaller enterprises. There are about 130 lots left of the original 450, and these will surely be sold by next year. The rise in prices in the next few months will be from thirty to fifty per cent. at the lowest estimate. South Ottumwa is now considered to be one of the most desirable residence portions of the city. Any inquiries will be promptly responded to by addressing Dr. W. B. Smith, 350 Ward St., South Ottumwa. Iowa.

Of Dr. W. B. Smith much could be said personally, as he stands high in the estimation of the citizens of two cities. Although a resident of Ann Arbor, he spends a great share of his time in South Ottumwa. He was born in Barre Centre, N. Y., in 1838, living there until nineteen, when he moved to Michigan with his father. He is a graduate of the medical department of the University of Michigan, class of '61. A year later he was commissioned assistant surgeon to the First Michigan Engineers and Mechanics Infantry, going through the war in Tennessee, Kentucky and Virginia with them. At the close of the war he returned to Ann Arbor and continued the practice of medicine. Although a republican, he has been elected mayor three times in the Democratic city of Ann Arbor. He has been on the school board of that city fifteen years, and is chairman of the committee on teachers and text-books, is a director in one of the banks, and besides an extensive practice in medicine and surgery, has a large farm to look after. In Ann Arbor he has platted one of that city's most beautiful additions. He is a prominent Mason, Knight Templar and Shriner. In South Ottumwa Dr. Smith is looked upon as the leading spirit in all movements. The very history of that thriving place is so closely interwoven with his life that the two are almost synonymous. When the Coal Palace fund was being subscribed, Dr. Smith raised $750, of which he subscribed $315 himself. They gave him their proxies, and of the twenty-two names proposed from which to choose thirteen directors, his was the fourth one elected. He was appointed chairman of the committee on reception and entertainments, and served on the building and printing committees. Dr. Smith possesses beneath a mild and gentle exterior, wonderful reserve force, determination, and strength of character, all of which is attested by his patriotism and untiring efforts in advancing the interests of South Ottumwa. No private vices, no public corruptions, have dimmed the lustre of his career, which promises to continue for many years of usefulness and public service.

2011 edition

MORRIS J. WILLIAMS. — One of the oldest and most respected citizens of South Ottumwa is Ex-Judge Morris J. Williams, who moved here in the fall of 1854, from Indiana, where he was born in 1829. He practiced law in Indiana, and was prosecuting attorney for Decatur and Rush counties part of the time. For five years he was Judge of the second judicial district of Iowa. In the discharge of his duties he knew neither friend nor foe, and his decisions were noted for their firmness and precision. At present Judge Williams devotes considerable time to a beautiful stock farm within the city limits, close to South Ottumwa, of which he is very proud. Here he bestows much care and attention in the breeding of fine horses. He made four additions to South Ottumwa from property owned by him and previously used for farm purposes, and they are beautiful and desirable tracts for residence sites.

4. Hon. Morris D. Williams.

REV. FRANCIS J. WARD, the Pastor of the Catholic Parish in South Ottumwa, was born in County Langford, Ireland. His early studies were pursued at St. Bernard's school, and in the French and German colleges at Black Rock, Dublin. He spent six years in St. Patrick's Ecclesiastical College at Carlow, Ireland, and June 9, 1879, was ordained for the priesthood.

He was immediately sent to this country and arrived in Ottumwa in 1880. The following year he secured lots from Mr. W. B. Smith, and in 1882 built the present church, shown in our illustrations, at a cost of about $10,000. The parochial residence was erected in 1884, at a cost of $3,500. It is of brick with stone trimmings and slate roof, and very pleasing architecturally. The large congregation at South Ottumwa numbers about one hundred and sixty families. Father Ward has a charge at Sigourney, Keokuk county, as well, where he has built a nice little church. In June, of this year, Father Ward started on a much-needed vacation to "the land where the Shamrock grows," and remained there until October, visiting many of the principal cities and points of interest. A more beloved or popular pastor than Father Ward does not live. By his kindness and charity he has made legions of firm and devoted friends.

Ottumwa 1890

C.T. Hartman home - S. Moore

C. T. HARTMAN, one of the most energetic and enterprising of the leading spirits of South Ottumwa, is a manufacturer of spring wagons, in connection with which he does a general blacksmithing and horseshoeing business. He has been a resident and business man of Ottumwa for fifteen years, moving to the south side eight years ago. He was born in Clayton county, Iowa. One of the heaviest real estate owners in South Ottumwa, he is ever ready to lend a helping hand to any enterprise rebounding in her favor. He has just commenced a two-story brick addition to his wagon works that will give him more room and enable him to supply the increasing demands for his manufactures. It will contain in the second story an extensive paint shop for painting, varnishing and finishing wagons. He is also owner of other buildings, both in Ottumwa and South Ottumwa, and has just completed the attractive residence shown among the illustrations. Mr. Hartman, although a young man, has served a term as city treasurer of Ottumwa, is highly respected by everyone, and always a contributor to charities and projects conducive to public progress and welfare.

Wm. Amelang home - S. Ransom Street

WM. AMELANG, Manufacturer of and Wholesale and Retail Dealer in Fine Harness and Saddles, 821 South Green street. The present prosperity and business activity of South Ottumwa are due to such enterprising men as Mr. Amelang and others. To show the spirit and enterprise of its merchants, such men as Mr. Amelang need only be mentioned; there is absolutely nothing carried in the harness and saddlery business that can not be found in his stock or made in his factory. He manufactures and handles as fine goods as any house in Iowa, and by reason of owning his own store can undersell all his competitors. He has been in the business for himself about thirteen years, and his strict honesty, together with the superiority of his goods, has always been a matter of common understanding among his thousands of customers. He owns a considerable amount of property in South Ottumwa, which he has had the pleasure of seeing grow very rapidly in value each year. We are glad of the privilege of calling public attention to Mr. Amelang, and only regret that space will not allow us to give him a more extended notice.

Ottumwa 1890

LLOYD FINLEY, Dealer in Lumber, located on the corner of Church and Davis streets, is conducting one of the most successful yards in the city. He is an old resident of the city, but a new star in the mercantile firmament. As one of the most progressive and thoroughly enterprising business men in the city, he is deserving of special mention in this work. He is one of the few shrewd and far-seeing men who realize that South Ottumwa will some day lead her Siamese sister across the river, and has driven his stakes in that growing portion of the city. He carries a stock of lumber equal to all demands, and of the finest and best the market affords. His trade is rapidly increasing, and he finds it necessary to employ four competent men to fill his orders for lumber. An honorable, upright gentleman, popular with all classes, his future success is certain and sure. A portrait of Mr. Finley appears on another page.

T. E. GIBBONS, Dealer in Imported and Domestic Staple and Fancy Groceries, 838 South Green street: Mr. Gibbons is one of South Ottumwa's leading and popular business men. A man endowed with great force of character, possessed of a liberal education and marked natural ability, coupled with a retentive memory and great mind for details, he has easily won for himself a conspicuous position in the political, as well as mercantile world of Ottumwa. For three years Mr. Gibbons represented his ward in the city council, being one of its most active and honored members. Of his business career it may be mentioned that he has been in the grocery trade for twenty years, and has conducted it with the greatest success.

T.E. Gibbons' Grocery

Shaw Steam Laundry wagon

W. S. RUSSELL, Proprietor of Shaw Steam Laundry, 1115 Church street. Mr. Russell conducts a thoroughly first-class laundry ; in fact his laundry is second to none in Iowa in point of completeness for the turning out of the finest work. He has all the modern machinery known to the business and employs none but the most experienced help. His foreman, W. C. Martin, was for four years in the employ of the Munger Steam Laundry of Des Moines, Iowa, the largest laundry in the state, and with the Des Moines steam laundry one year. Mr. Russell guarantees his work equal to any done in Chicago—and the writer of this article knows his work to be all he claims for it. He came here in 1880 from Eldon, Iowa, where he was engaged in the dry goods business for four years. He is a man of superior ability, a thorough business man, gentlemanly, courteous and pleasing in manners, whom everybody respects. A splendid picture of his delivery wagon, which is the finest equipage of its kind in Ottumwa, appears on another page, and is as fine as anything in the state. More delivery wagons are employed but space will not permit representing them.

Ottumwa 1890

OTTUMWA CIGAR BOX FACTORY, 401 South Green street, is one of the largest concerns of its kind in the West. It was established by its present proprietor Mr. A. S. Cook, January 1, 1888. He is an experienced man at the business, and turns out as fine work as any done in the East. He employs eleven experienced workmen, a number that will be rapidly increased, inasmuch as the orders at present are far ahead of the supply. Mr. Cook keeps one traveling salesman out continuously, who visits the principal cities in Iowa and Missouri. The factory turns out at present one thousand cigar boxes per day, but by a large addition to the building this number will be doubled. Three machines capable of nailing these boxes are kept in constant motion. They are a novelty in mechanism, all they require being four pieces of board, which, being handed them, they will return made into a box and securely nailed. Mr. Cook is one of the most progressive young men in Ottumwa, and a man whom everybody respects and admires.

Ottumwa Cigar Box Factory, South Green Street

A. J. PECK, 802-804 South Green street, owns and operates one of the largest and finest livery, feed and sale stables in Ottumwa. His fine new building, a cut of which is herein presented, is located on the South side, one block from the river, and on the leading business street of that portion of the city. The street railway passes the building and telephone connection is made with all the hotels of the city. Mr. Peck keeps a large stable of excellent horses, and his carriages, landaus, coupes, etc., are all new and very fine. His stables for years have been headquarters for horsemen, and now, with his new building, his facilities in this direction are greatly increased, especially as he is surrounded by all the mills and shops of the south side. The undertaking business is also one of his features, and he has houses, furniture and musical

A.J. Peck Livery Stable, 802-804 South Green

instruments to rent. One of the windows of his block is occupied by a handsome art display from the studio of Mrs. A. J. Peck, who teaches embroidery and "lightning" painting, French hand-made flowers and decorative work. Her paintings have taken the first premium at most of the surrounding fairs, and at the Agency fair alone she has captured nine first premiums. Mr. Peck was born and raised here and he owes his present comfortable fortune, in a large measure, to the growth and prosperity of Ottumwa, having early made extensive investments in real estate. He is well known and universally respected.

Ottumwa 1890

PUTNAM & BRIDGEMAN, Retail Notions, Crockery, Glassware, Tinware, Queensware, School Supplies, Stationery, Books, Hardware, Toys, etc., etc. This is the famous five and ten-cent store which has paralyzed the trade of other stores handling the same line of goods. Every article in their large store is of superior quality, and when one recalls the prices they have paid for similar articles in the past, of the same grade and make, they are surprised and can not understand how goods can be sold for such a sum as five and ten cents. No article in their store, here or at other points, is sold for more than ten cents, notwithstanding the fact that many of them are sold by other dealers for from twenty-five to fifty cents. A clear idea of the money to be saved by purchasing goods of this house may be gained from the mention of a few of their goods and prices. They sell a large stew kettle, retinned, for ten cents, four-quart sauce pan ten cents, ten-quart milk pan ten cents, full-sized house broom ten cents, washboard ten cents, fine wood pipe ten cents, extra fine whisk broom ten cents, steel butcher knife ten cents, double mincing knife ten cents, tea canister ten cents, full-sized hatchet ten cents, feather duster ten cents, hair curler ten cents, and thousands of other articles for five and ten cents. Every housekeeper should call and examine this stock of goods before making purchases elsewhere. Putnam & Bridgeman have stores at Peoria, Ill.; Adrian, Mich.; Fostoria, Ohio. These connections, and the fact that they buy all their goods direct from the manufacturers in large quantities, makes the secret of their prices plain to all.

For the holiday trade they have purchased five thousand dollars worth of toys and presents of all kinds, both useful and ornamental, which, added to their present immense stock, will make it the largest and most complete of any in the city or state. Those unable to visit the store should send for their catalogue. Mr. Bridgeman has charge of the business here.

2011 edition

Wm. B. Armstrong home - 440 N. Jefferson

WM. B. ARMSTRONG, local freight agent of the C. B. & Q. Railway. Although not engaged in mercantile or manufacturing pursuits, Mr. Armstrong is richly deserving of mention in this book, by reason of his activity and deep interest in all things pertaining to the material interests of the city. The public schools are objects of deep solicitude to him and he never allows an opportunity to pass whereby he could add to their strength, influence or popularity. He recognizes in them the only assurance of a free republican form of government for future generations—the permanency of and addition to our present public institutions. Mr. Armstrong was born in Pennsylvania, August 10, 1830. He received a good education in the schools of Sussex county, New Jersey. Upon completion of his studies he decided to see the West, and leaving home traveled across the country to St. Louis, where he secured a clerical position with a commission house, remaining with them a number of years. From St. Louis he went to Athens, Mo., where he received the appointment as local agent of the Keokuk, Des Moines & Minnesota Railroad, a position he held for eleven years. In 1861 he came to Ottumwa where he acted in the same capacity for the company until 1872, when he resigned to accept his present position with the C. B. & Q. Company. He is considered one of the best posted men in railway business in the west. He is an honored member of Blue Lodge Chapter and Commandery of Masons; is a republican; has held several public offices, among them being a term or two as alderman, six years as school director and two terms as city treasurer.

Ottumwa 1890

OTTUMWA BOILER WORKS, C. B. McDaniel, proprietor, is one of the largest concerns of its kind in Iowa. The best evidence of the great superiority of the McDaniel boilers is found in the fact that they are in constant use in such well known establishments as the Morrell & Co., pork packing house, Ottumwa Starch Mills, Johnston Ruffler Co. Shops, Ottumwa Linseed Oil Mills, Electric Street R'y, Steam heat and Power Co., Whitebreast Fuel Co., What Cheer Coal Co., Creston Coal Co., and hundreds of others, all through the States of Iowa, Missouri, Illinois, Kansas, Nebraska, Colorado and Washington. Mr. McDaniel employs a very large force of the most skilled workmen, and aside from the construction of boilers he makes all kinds of heavy iron work, engine castings and general mill supplies. Mr. McDaniel is so thoroughly well known to residents of Ottumwa and the state that it seems unnecessary to speak of him personally, but for the benefit of those who may not know him and who may wish to deal with him, we will say that he has the reputation of being an honorable, upright business man. He enjoys the respect and confidence of all who know him.

Consolidated Tank Line

THE CONSOLIDATED TANK LINE COMPANY was established in Ottumwa in 1882. Mr. J. G. Howard, the popular manager, of this large branch establishment has been with the company nine years and has had charge of the warehousers and business here since its inception. Three immense tanks are used for storing refined oil and gasoline from which one dray wagon and one tank wagon are constantly drawing oil for distribution among the hundreds of customers in the city, while many car loads in barrels are shipped to different points in Iowa and Missouri. Mr. Howard is the right man in the right place, he is liked by all who meet him, and the growth of the business here attests his ability to meet all demands of employers and customers alike. Mr. A. A. Myers is Mr. Howard's able and popular assistant manager.

UNION IRON WORKS AND STEAM HEATING Co., Corner Main and Wapello streets. This establishment is one of the largest and most successful in the state. They manufacture steam engines, steam-pumps, steam heating apparatus, plumbers' supplies, etc. Their specialty is brass goods of all kinds, and their strongest feature is fine steam and hot water heating. None but the most skilled and experienced workmen are employed, and as a consequence the firm turns out none but the very highest grade of work, and the same can not be excelled by any firm or company in the United States. Their goods go to Missouri, Kansas, Minnesota, Nebraska and all parts of Iowa. Every article manufactured is guaranteed to be of the highest standard of workmanship. The members of the firm are : E. B. Wise, Thomas Turner, H. P. Keyhoe and William Stirling. Mr. Wise was for ten years with the Johnston Ruffler Co., two years as foreman, and is considered to-day one of the leading men in his line in this country. Mr. Turner, a new addition to the firm, is a man ripe in experience, and late with the Johnston Ruffler Co., where he has been for the past five years. Mr. Keyhoe is a practical machinist of long experience. He was employed in the shops of two of the largest concerns in this city for eight years. He represents the fourth ward in the city council and  is a trustworthy and faithful representative. Mr. Stirling has had most of his experience in the cities of Boston and Chicago. Altogether he has had twenty years' experience, and is considered a graduate in his trade. All members of the firm are men of exceptional business ability and of excellent character and integrity. They are furnishing steam heating for the largest buildings throughout this and adjoining states, and as evidence of their standing in Ottumwa it is only necessary to mention a few of their most prominent contracts, viz.—New Opera House, Baker Bros., Lilburn & Co., Chas. O. Taylor, Chas. Bachman, Geo. O. Brown, Henry Throne, Dr. C. O. Lewis, David Throne, W. R. Daum, First Baptist church, Presbyterian church, St. Mary's Catholic church, Rev. John Kreckel's residence, and First National bank.

Ottumwa 1890

J. T. WEIR & SON, dealers in flour, feed, paints, oils, varnishes, lime and cement, have their large store and warehouse at 116 to 118 East Second street. The business was established in 1879 by Cooper & Weir, and changed to Weir & Son in 1887. Mr. J. T. Weir has had forty years' experience in the lime and cement business and twelve years in the flour and feed business. He is a citizen who commands the respect and esteem of all who know him. His long business career in Ottumwa has not been tarnished by any acts of dishonesty— not even by a single unbusiness-like transaction—in public or private life. Robt. D. Weir, the son, is following closely in his father's footsteps, being greatly respected by all who know him as an honest, upright and conscientious young man. He is bright, wide-awake, and progressive, capable of managing any business in which he might engage. He is enterprising and always ready to liberally aid all projects that give promise of advancing the material welfare of the city. Of the business of Weir & Son it can be said that they carry one of the heaviest stocks of goods, in each of their lines in the state. They sell goods at wholesale and retail, and are always prepared to fill any order sent them at the lowest market prices.

Turner Halle Opera House - later the site of the Armory building, Market & Fourth

2011 edition

Taylor Block - Main and Court

TAYLOR & COMPANY, Druggists, Dealers in Books, Stationery, Wall Paper, Curtains, Imported and Domestic Cigars, Wholesale and Retail, are located on the corner of Main and Court streets, occupying the largest and finest rooms in the city, being fifty by seventy-five feet. The stock of goods carried by this firm is one of the largest, finest and most complete of any in Iowa or the West. They are the leaders in the drug, book, stationery, wall paper and cigar business of Ottumwa. Occupying their own building, they have no rent to pay, and are thus enabled to undersell all competitors. A number of physicians have their offices on the upper floors of their building and others near by, which, together with the central location of the store, gives them the largest prescription trade in the city. Their drugs and chemicals are always fresh and warranted full strength. Their line of books, wall paper, etc., is the finest in the city, while their stock of imported and domestic cigars cannot be duplicated outside of Chicago. The history of this business dates from 1860. The present members of the firm are—Chas. O. Taylor, W. D. Elliott, and G. A. Warden, Mr. Taylor being a son of the original founder of the business. The constantly increasing business of the house is evidence of the popularity of the proprietors, their superior ability and straightforward, honorable methods of conducting it.

Ottumwa 1890

JULIUS FECHT, manufacturer of and wholesale dealer in cigar and tobacco, 211 and 213 South Market street. Mr. Fecht is well known to dealers in fine cigars and tobacco throughout Iowa, northern Missouri, Kansas, Nebraska and South Dakota as the manufacturer of some of the finest brands of domestic cigars placed upon the western market. He has had twenty years' experience, and, as a consequence, cannot be excelled as a judge of quality and workmanship. He gives the business his close and constant attention and no goods leave his factory which he does not personally know are equal to the standard so long maintained by him. Mr. Fecht believes in manufacturing an article which will sell itself, after once thoroughly introduced, in competition with all others; and as an evidence that he can accomplish this, he sends out but one traveling salesman, yet his factory turns out in the neighborhood of one million cigars annually. Mr. Fecht is a splendid business man, and he enjoys the confidence and respect of all men who come in contact with him in a business or social way.

Works of Ottumwa Cutlery Co. -
located at 214 -218 S. Tisdale

HON. W. W. EPPS, the Mayor of Ottumwa, is one of the leading lawyers of the state and one of her most honored and respected citizens. He was born in Ohio in 1854, taught school ten years: was admitted to the bar in 1880, and practiced four years in Ohio. He came to Ottumwa in 1884. He served two years as city attorney, was chairman of the Republican State Central Committee for one year previous to his election as mayor. His success in his law practice, like that in teaching, has been almost phenomenal. A man of great moral courage, a fearless, able debater, and a man of commanding presence, he inspires confidence in all with whom he comes in contact. He is jovial, entertaining and attractive. Being a man of great learning, keen perception, quick at repartee, polished in manners and speech, he becomes a shining light in any company in which he finds himself placed. His natural gifts, coupled with his ability as a lawyer and scholar, must sooner or later place him in a prominent position among the leading men of the nation. His duties as the executive officer of the city have been performed with all the fidelity of an honorable man. During his administration more has been done in the way of improvements than was ever before accomplished in the same length of time, and has resulted in making him the most popular officer in the city. He is a member of the following civic societies: Grand Lodge, Knights of Pythias, Head Camp, Modern Woodmen of America, and Royal Arcanum. He is sergeant of Company G, I. N. G., a member of the rifle team and a crack shot.

3. Hon. W. W. Epps.

Ottumwa 1890

1. W. H. Boston.

W. H. BOSTON, 108 South Court street, Manufacturer and Wholesale Dealer in Harness and Saddles, begun [sic] business here in 1879, and in the eleven years that have elapsed he has outstripped all competitors, and to-day has a trade second to none in the west outside of Chicago. His goods are the equal, in point of quality and workmanship, of any made in this or a foreign country, and their reputation as such is so well established that no competitor can secure any of his customers. His goods go to all the principal points in Iowa, Nebraska, Kansas and Montana. In making single-track harness and turf goods he has no superior. In fact, this applies to everything used or worn by horses. He guarantees satisfaction or no sale, and his references as to honesty and character are the finest. An order sent to him will bear out the truth of these statements.

7. G. H. Sheffer.

G. H. SHEFFER, one of the leading dry goods merchants of the city, was born in Nova Scotia, January 6, 1834. His early life was spent in Boston, where he acquired his education. For a number of years he was engaged in the lumber business in Maine, conducting it with splendid success. In 1862 he sold out his lumber business and removed to Ottumwa, where for eleven years he was the proprietor of one of the largest dry goods houses in the city, which he disposed of in 1873 and entered the house of Jordan & Sons where he remained until 1879, when he went into business again for himself. He has just moved into his new store at 228 E. Main street, one of the lightest and most elegant establishments in the city. Mr. Sheffer is conspicuous as a successful business man of superior ability, standing high in the confidence and esteem of the people of Southern Iowa. His portrait appears on another page. He served two terms in the city council, and although he has been renominated several times he has refused to accept.

THRALL & GEPHART, retail grocers, 103 East Second street. Frank B. Thrall and Walter Gephart associated themselves in this business in the latter part of 1889. Both are active, energetic young men who have always been popular and highly esteemed members of Ottumwa society. Their success was assured from the day they opened their handsome store. Mr. Thrall has had many years' experience as a traveling salesman for the wholesale grocery firm of J. H. Merrill & Co. He stands high as a Knight of Pythias and is Chancellor Commander of Wappello [sic] Lodge, No. 12, Ottumwa. Mr. Gephart is a druggist and chemist by profession, and for many years was connected with his brother's drug store on Main street. He is a member of the Masonic fraternity. Judging from the enterprise of the firm, thus far displayed, they will soon be in possession of as large a patronage as is enjoyed by any retail grocery store in the city or state. Both members of the firm were born and raised in this county, and they have the esteem and fullest confidence of the entire community. They have both travelled extensively all over this country, and after visiting and doing business in many of the largest western cities they have returned with the confidence that Ottumwa is good enough for them.

The Fair, located at 416 E. Main Street, was operated by Jacob Ferber, the father of well-known novelist Edna Ferber.

Ottumwa 1890

J. C. FORKEL & Co., wholesale and retail dealers in game of all kinds, fresh fish and oysters, 323 East Main street. This firm handles more fish, game and oysters than any other similar concern in southern Iowa. Mr. Forkel came here from Rochester, N. Y., in 1880, and for four years was steward of the Ballingall House, afterwards becoming manager of Cripps & Bro.'s transfer business.

6. J. C. Forkel.

Mr. Forkel's father opened the first wholesale and retail oyster establishment in Rochester, N. Y., and for six years J. C. Forkel was connected with it before coming west. He is well known to the merchants of the city as an honorable, upright business man, worthy of the confidence and respect of all who may have business relations with him. He is a man of superior business ability, and there can be no doubt of his success in this new venture. The firm will be represented by a number of traveling salesmen on the road to cover the surrounding territory. They are sole agents for the celebrated Heinsen & Co.'s "Square" Brand of Baltimore oysters, which they will dispose of in wholesale and retail quantities. Any inquiry by mail or wire will be promptly attended to, and a trial order from this new house will convince any new customer that he is dealing with an enterprising and honorable firm.

W. B. WYCOFF & SON, real estate and loan brokers, Richard's block, 128 East Main street. This is one of the leading, thoroughly reliable real estate and loan firms of Ottumwa. By the strictest integrity they have acquired the confidence of all classes. Mr. W. B. Wycoff has been long familiar with all lands in this and adjoining counties, having located here in 1846, and, consequently, is familiar with every foot of land in the city from its center to its boundaries. His knowledge of values is unsurpassed by anyone in the city. He has had long and successful experience in both buying and selling real estate. Mr. J. C. Wycoff is one of Ottumwa's youngest business men and one of the most energetic and prosperous. Both have farms in this and adjoining counties, and they know just what a good farm is and take great pains and care to suit every customer. They always have a large list of farms and city property on their books, and they feel confident they can suit anyone wanting to make an investment in real estate for a home or as an investment. Be sure to call on them, you will be courteously and kindly treated. References, by permission — First National, Ottumwa National and Iowa National Banks, all of this city.

6. W. B. Wycoff.

J.C. Wycoff

Ottumwa 1890

WALTER T. HALL, Manufacturing Confectioner, Jobber in Crackers and Foreign Nuts, 131—133 Third street. From a modest beginning in 1878 has sprung one of the largest manufacturing and jobbing houses in the entire west outside of Chicago. But it is not for the great number and extent of their sales that this house is conspicuous so much as it is for the superior excellence of their goods. It is certainly impossible to make the reader understand, however great our effort, in what way and how this firm's goods are superior to others. But the fact

5. Walter T. Hall.

remains that no confections manufactured in this or any foreign country meet with greater public favor than those from Mr. Hall's factory. We can only say to the dealers throughout the country, east, west, north or south, try them once and you will carry no others in stock. Mr. Hall keeps four traveling salesmen on the road continuously; their orders, however, represent but a small portion of those received and filled. One order to this house brings more, whether a representative of the house calls on the dealer or not. The business is rapidly increasing, and with each succeeding year more room and more help become an imperative necessity. In crackers and nuts, Mr. Hall handles none but the very finest the market affords, and never ships a bill of them which he does not personally know are in first class condition and as good as can be obtained in any market. Of Mr. Hall personally no more need be said than a mention of the fact that he has lived here many years of his life, during which time he has proven himself worthy of the entire confidence esteem of all who have had intercourse with him in business, either public or private. He is a man of marked ability and a generous, public-spirited citizen.

2011 edition

J.W. Garner home - 424 E. Second

F. M. HUNTER & Co., druggists, 308 E. Main street—Ballingall Hotel Pharmacy. This is one of the very finest and coziest, as well as oldest drug stores in Ottumwa. In its prescription department it enjoys a trade excelled by none, and is the favorite resort of many of the leading physicians of the city. The management of the store is entrusted to Mr. F. B. Clark, a young man of social popularity and winning business manners. He has lived in Ottumwa for three years, having practiced his profession for ten years and is a graduate of the Illinois College of Pharmacy at Chicago. He is assisted by Mr. W. L. Sargent, a registered pharmacist with six years' experience, a very bright and promising young business man of engaging appearance and address. One of the most complete stocks of fine imported and domestic cigars kept on hand anywhere, is to be found here. A magnificent assortment of perfumery extracts, toilet articles of all kinds and druggists' sundries is temptingly displayed. The furnishing of the store is the most elegant and substantial of any in Ottumwa, as may be seen in the illustration of the interior in this volume. A costly and beautiful soda fountain is one of the chief ornaments of the store. The firm stands high in the estimation of the people of Ottumwa as enterprising factors of the city's improvement and advancement. They purchased the store in June, 1890, and have done much to increase its popularity and patronage in the short space of time they have had control of it. Both are men who strive to please the public and both have won by straightforward and courteous business methods many warm and devoted friends.

Ottumwa 1890

J. W. NORRIS, located at 218 South Market street, is engaged in the upholstery and poultry business, which he conducts separately but in the same building. He opened his two houses in the early part of 1890 since which time he has done a successful business that is gradually assuming large proportions. He is an enterprising young man of more than ordinary ability that knows how to hustle for trade, and he is making his influence felt by the old and long established houses in both branches of his business. He has had an experience in the upholstering business extending over many years and in nearly every large city in the Union. He ships poultry to Chicago and purchases all his upholstering material from Marshall Field & Co. Mr. Norris has made many warm friends during the short time he has been in business here by his pleasant manners and kind treatment of all who have come in contact with him. He is deserving of success, and he is enjoying his full share of it.

J. G. SMITH & CO., dealers in new and second-hand merchandise, 315 E. Main street. Mr. Smith is conspicuous among those who have always willingly contributed to enterprises for the benefit of the city; appreciating the benefits and advantages derived from judiciously advertising Ottumwa to the outside world. Mr. Smith was born in Virginia and when but one year of age became, unconsciously, an emigrant with his father to Ohio, where he resided until he came to Ottumwa, in 1861. His first occupation was teaching school at Agency, afterwards at Dahlonega and in Ottumwa. He was a carpenter by trade, but became the leading house-mover of this city, following that line for years. In his present business he has been engaged for about twenty years. He is a greatly respected and popular citizen.

J. N. ARMSTRONG, one of the very foremost dentists in Ottumwa, occupies handsome quarters at 213 E. Main street. He has been in the active practice of his profession for fifteen years; two years at Burlington, three years at Sigourney, Iowa, and ten years in Ottumwa, where he has built up an extensive practice extending all over the state. Socially Dr. Armstrong is greatly respected. Still a young man, affable and pleasing in manners, he has a bright and prosperous future before him.

Drug Store of F. M. Hunter & Co.

Ottumwa 1890

THE BAKER HOUSE, under the proprietorship of one of the best fellows in the world, S. M. Stancliff, is the only first-class hostelry, with the exception of the Ballingall, in Ottumwa. Never, since its erection in 1880 has it been so popular or so well patronized as under the present management. This is due to the geniality of its landlord, the attractive manner of serving meals, the excellence of the cooking, and the genuine comfort of its beds. It is a well known fact, especially among hotel men, that the traveling public care but little for imposing hotel structures, royal furnishings and stiff, dignified servants if not accompanied by well cooked, attractively served meals and clean white table and bed linen. Mr. Stancliff has made his reputation as one of the best hotel men in the west by giving his guests a bill of fare made up from the choicest viands afforded by the markets, cooked and served to please the most fastidious tastes and by the most painstaking care of his guest chambers; the linen is always white and fresh and the rooms clean, bright and inviting. Mr. Stancliff bought out the former proprietor of the Baker House in 1889, and as soon as given possession refitted, renovated, and refurnished it from top to bottom, making it first-class in every particular. There are forty sleeping apartments aside from the private rooms, parlors and reception rooms. The dining-room is light, airy and spacious, seating from one to two hundred people without inconvenience. From twenty to thirty servants find employment in the house. Of Mr. Stancliff nothing further need be said than to mention his great popularity with the traveling public and to state that he is a young man of progressive ideas. He enjoys high standing in business

Office and rotunda of the Baker House - located at 218 - 224 S. Green

circles and possesses the confidence and esteem of all who know him. Next spring there will be alterations and additions that will doubly increase the present capacity, and no expense will be spared to make the Baker House one of the most attractive in the west.

Dining room of the Baker House

J. H. RHEEM, 117 East Main street, is the leading music dealer of the city. He carries the largest stock of music and musical instruments in southern Iowa. Mr. Rheem was professor of music in the public schools of Carlisle, Penn., before coming to Iowa. Previous to removing to this city in 1882, he was professor of music in the public schools of Chariton, Iowa, and afterwards of the public schools of Oskaloosa, Iowa, a position which he has since filled in Ottumwa, with the greatest success and to the entire satisfaction of the school board, the scholars and the public. He is the agent here for the following world celebrated lines of pianos: Chickering, Decker Bros., Wheelock & Schubert. Also keeps a large stock of Estey and Chicago Cottage Organs, and a general line of sheet music, and musical merchandise of all kinds.

Ottumwa 1890

THE B. B. SHIRT FACTORY, 319 East Main street, is owned and conducted by Miss Kate Boughner, and is the only establishment of the kind in Ottumwa. Miss Boughner has had ten years' experience in the manufacture of fine shirts, and most of that time was spent in the factory of that renowned shirt-maker E. M. Noble. That she can satisfy the most exacting is evidenced by the fact that she makes shirts for nearly all the doctors, editors and lawyers in Ottumwa. She made all the suits worn by the Ottumwa base ball team during the present season. Her specialty is fine dress shirts, and in the manufacture of these she acknowledges no superiors and but very few equals. She employs none but the most experienced shirt-makers and turns out about five hundred shirts per month. Miss Boughner anticipates moving into larger quarters before the coming of spring, as her present location is much too small to keep up with her increasing business.

Kate D. Boughner.

J. J. Bowles.

J. J. BOWLES, Dealer in Fruits, Oysters, Confections, etc., is one of the best merchants and caterers of the city having been in business here since 1870. He has recently moved into handsome new quarters at 312 East Main street, which he has fitted up in artistic style. Mr. Bowles makes a specialty of choice California and Tropical fruits. In the winter season the oyster trade occupies his attention. As a Caterer, Mr. Bowles is acknowledged to be one of the most successful in the country, and orders for serving wedding suppers, banquets, etc., come to him without solicitation.

CHAS. BACHMAN, Wholesale and Retail Jeweler, 210 East Main street, is one of the substantial business men of Ottumwa, who has very materially aided the city to grow and prosper. Mr. Bachman has been in business here for twenty-two years, and has, during that time, built up a wholesale and retail trade second to none west of Chicago. His stock of diamonds, watches and silver goods is very large and always replete with all the latest styles and novelties of the season. He keeps two men on the road who make the principal cities in Iowa and adjoining states, and who find no difficulty in holding trade against the active competition of Chicago houses. Goods purchased of this house are sure to give satisfaction, as Mr. Bachman's guarantee is a safe-guard against an inferior article.

S. C. CULLEN & Co., Dry Goods, 130 East Main street. This is one of the leading as well as the largest dry goods houses in Ottumwa. The members of the firm are, Miss Sadie C. Cullen and H. A. Warner. The store is conspicuous for two things, first and foremost of which is its attractiveness in its large display of the freshest, newest goods in all the latest styles and novelties. Everything near to the feminine heart in the line of dress goods, from the daintiest laces to the most expensive and elegant silks, satins, etc., are always to be found in this store. A secondary reason for its conspicuousness is found in the fact that it is conducted by a lady. It is not often that a lady is found at the head of so large an establishment. But Miss Cullen is not a tyro in this line, as she managed the dry goods store of Israel Bros., for five years previous to her going into business for herself. She goes to New York twice each year to purchase goods, and the large patronage the store enjoys speaks for her good taste and judgment. Mr. Warner, the company of the firm, is a well known and highly respected member of the traveling fraternity, representing an extensive New York dry goods house. Mr. Frank Cullen is in the store with his sister; also Miss Davis, formerly with Israel Bros.

Ottumwa 1890

E. G. YONGE & Bro., Bakers, Wholesale and Retail. One of the leading bakeries in Ottumwa is that of E. G. Yonge & Bro., located at 402 East Main street. This prominent concern was established in 1865 by the present firm, E. G. and J. G. Yonge. It has enjoyed a splendid patronage from the day of its opening up to the present and has grown in public favor and patronage until to-day it is one of the largest concerns of the kind in the city or state. The firm employs eight thoroughly experienced hands and keeps two traveling salesmen on the road. They guarantee that their goods and their prices are as low as is consistent for high grade quality and workmanship. They do a large wholesale business in the city and throughout all portions of the state. They consume ten to twelve barrels and upwards of flour per day and bake from one to two thousand loaves of bread in that time. In the manufacture of sweet goods, such as jumbles and fancy cakes, they lead all others, as their machinery is the very latest improved. Their facilities for shipping goods is the best in the city and they are able to fill orders in the least possible time.

F. H. FIELDS, retail jeweler, 218 East Main street, is one of the most enterprising and progressive jewelers and silverware dealers of Ottumwa. While not occupying as much space as some other dealers, he succeeds in securing his full share of public patronage. He has had many years' experience in the watch-making and jewelry business, having worked at the trade in the large watch factory at Elgin, Ill., with another firm at Atlantic, Iowa, and for himself at Newton, Kan., making in all fourteen years' experience in the business. He employs no apprentices, personally doing all work entrusted to him. Mr. Field is very popular among his customers and associates, making many warm friends by his upright business methods and pleasing, affable manners.

F. S. CUMMINGS, Boots and Shoes, 114 Main street. Mr. Cummings is one of Ottumwa's most prominent and substantial young business men. For six years he was in the boot and shoe business in Fairfield, Iowa, but becoming satisfied that Ottumwa is destined to be the largest city in the state, he has decided to locate here permanently. By his push, energy and modern business methods he has secured a commanding position in the mercantile world of Ottumwa. Every purchaser of goods in his store is given a ticket that entitles the holder to a chance to draw a fine parlor organ. The previous prize was a beautiful solid gold watch. His stock is from the leading factories of this country, such as Thos. Boulton, Gray Bros., Baldwin & Lamkin and others. Mr. Cummings is assisted by two very efficient salesmen, Messrs. Arthur H. Lewis and Will Potter, who are among the most popular of the young men of the city, both in business and social circles. Connected with this house is one of the finest shoemakers in the country, Mr. William Dinklage, a native of Germany, who has been in this country four years. He has had thirteen years' experience and is a thoroughly first-class workman.

H. R. VANDERCOOK,   P. N. TUCKER.

VANDERCOOK & CO.,

ENGRAVERS AND ILLUSTRATORS,

WOOD ENGRAVING, ZINC ETCHING

AND HALF TONE,

409 to 415 Dearborn Street,
(DONOHUE & HENNEBERRY BUILDING)

Correspondence Solicited.   CHICAGO, ILL.

Ottumwa 1890

J. A. Phillips' "Famous" Shoe Store

J. A. PHILLIPS, Famous Shoe Store, Wholesale and Retail dealer in boots and shoes. This is acknowledged to be the largest and finest boot and shoe house in the State of Iowa. The wholesale trade of the house extends over Iowa, Missouri and Nebraska, while the rsil trade is larger than that of any four other houses in the city. The proprietor of this establishment is entirely a self-made man. In 1884 he started in the shoe business in a modest and unassuming way with no established trade and no assurance of such a blessing. But he had something equal to it, a hopeful disposition backed by a pushing, enterprising spirit, strong will, and a determination to deal fairly and honestly with every customer. He proved steadfast to these principles, and they have rewarded him; he stands at the head of all competitors in his chosen pursuit. In May, 1890, Mr. Phillips purchased the large three-story and basement store, No. 214 East Main street, paying therefor the sum of $10,000, and expending $2,000 in making needed improvements. The ground floor, which is 22 by 150 feet, and

J.A. Phillips

extends from Main to Commercial street, is fitted up in elegant style for his retail trade, changing the front and putting in the largest plate glass window ever brought to the city. He has 3,500 feet of shelving in his retail department. Every convenience is afforded customers in the shape of toilet rooms, wash rooms, elevator, etc. A cut of the store and of Mr. Phillips appears on another page.

FRED SWENSON, Ottumwa's leading tailor, occupies a large store at 313 East Main street, where he displays the finest and largest stock of cloths carried by any house in the West, outside of Chicago. As a tailor Mr. Swenson can be classed with the leading tailors of New York, Boston and Philadelphia. He has had thirty-five years' experience in the tailoring business in this and foreign countries—thirteen in the old country and twenty-two in the United States. He came to Ottumwa in 1877 and opened his present store, which he has conducted uninterruptedly from that time up to the present. A man of splendid business ability, honorable and upright in all his dealings, he enjoys the confidence and respect of the people to an unusual degree. He is a thorough gentleman, affable and pleasing in manners and address, of a generous, charitable disposition, whom to know is to respect and admire, and who by his many exemplary traits of character has made for himself a legion of friends.

1. Fred Swenson.

SMITH & FIEDLER, Blank Book Manufacturers and Book Binders, 112 East Main street. This enterprising firm is furnishing work in their line to the citizens of Ottumwa, Iowa and adjoining states equal to any turned out by the trade in Chicago and at much lower prices. They have the facilities for doing all classes of blank book making and binding, and, with thirteen years' experience, certainly should be able to hold their own with any other bookmaking concern. They keep a large force of experienced hands and can turn out the largest orders in the shortest possible time. They keep two traveling salesmen on the road traveling over Iowa and Missouri. Their specialty is the making of county and bank supplies. Of the members of the firm, Chas. A. Smith and William Fiedler, whose portraits are shown in this book, nothing further need be said than that they are pushing young business men who stand high in the esteem and confidence of the people of Ottumwa, men of strict integrity, honorable and straightforward in all their dealings, respected by all.

J. F. LEWIS & SON are in the Real Estate, loan and Insurance business, at 234 East Main street. This business was established in 1880. The firm was originally Lewis & Criley, from which it changed to Lewis & Adler, and afterwards to Lewis & Son. They are too well known to citizens of Ottumwa to need any introduction or words of praise from the publishers of this book. Mr. J. F. Lewis was engaged in the dry goods and clothing business for twenty years, was deputy sheriff for three years, constable for five years and city marshal for one year, and is now alderman from his, the fifth ward. Mr. L. D. Lewis, like his father, is a wide-awake and enterprising citizen. The firm makes a specialty of real estate, both city and farm lands, owning and controlling some of the finest property, both inside and suburban, in the city. They also represent the following well known insurance companies: The Liberty, of New York; California, of San Francisco; Citizens', of Pittsburg [sic]; Fire and Marine, of Detroit; Denver, of Denver; Commercial, of California.

2011 edition

S. L. MCGAVIC LUMBER Co., dealers in Lumber, 216 South Jefferson street. The oldest as well as one of the largest lumber firms inOttumwa, if not in the state, is that of S. L. McGavic Lumber Co. Mr. McGavic has been in the lumber business since 1866 in other parts of the country. For a number of years the firm name was McGavic & Springer. The present "Co." is represented by Frank C. Warden, a well-known and highly respected young usiness man of the city. He was born and raised here. Mr. McGavic has lived in Ottumwa since 1876. A native of Ohio he has resided in Iowa since 1855. Mr. Warden was connected with J. H. Walker & Co., of Chicago, for two or three years. The firm carry a very large stock of thoroughly dried, selected lumber of all kinds. They make a specialty of the finest grades of California Redwood lumber and shingles. Estimates on bills of lumber are always promptly and cheerfully furnished. Their stock of prepared building paper is one of the largest and most complete of any in the city.

W. D. Elliot home - 415 N. Court

Ottumwa 1890

HARMAN & WARDEN, 224 East Main street. This is one of the largest and strongest fire insurance agencies in Iowa. The firm is composed of R. H. Warden and J. L. Harman. Mr. Warden is a native of Maysville, Ky., born in 1826. He learned the printer's trade in Ohio, and coming to Ottumwa, in 1849, he established the *Courier*. In 1849 he was appointed postmaster. August 18, 1862, he enlisted in Company E, 36th Iowa Volunteer Infantry, was elected First Lieutenant, and served two years and five months with the 7th Army Corps under Gen. E. O. C. Ord, Steele's Division. It was in the recruiting service in Iowa, in winters of 1863—4, that he made a phenomenal record. The record shows that he recruited 165 more men than any other officer in the state during the same length of time. He served as Aide-decamp to General Asboth and Gen. B. M. Prentiss, and Assistant Adjutant-general of the 2d Brigade, 1st Division of Steele's Army Corps. For several years he was Assistant Assessor of Internal Revenue, and was its gauger. From December, 1869, to April, 1890, he was associate editor and business manager of the *Daily Courier*. He has held various city offices.

Mr. Harman is a native of Ohio, and has lived in Ottumwa almost continuously since 1858. He served in the war with the 4th Indiana Cavalry, and at the close was with the 175th Ohio Infantry. Returning to this city he became deputy auditor for two years, and then went into the insurance business, which he has followed ever since.

Both members of the firm have been liberal contributors to all public enterprises which have done much to build up the city of their adoption and make it one of the leading cities of the state.

HENRY THRONE. Among the most attractive of our illustrations is the representation given the grocery store and residence combined of Henry Throne, corner of Second and McLean streets. Although an up-town grocer, Mr. Throne is the leader of all others in

Henry Throne residence and store

everything the term implies. He conducts a branch store, corner of Maple avenue and Court street, and deals in flour and feed, boots and shoes, and fancy and staple groceries. His store, as illustrated, is not only the finest in Ottumwa, but it is the most artistic and pleasing west of Chicago. The writer has visited many of the principal cities in this country and he can truly say that Mr. Throne has exhibited finer taste and more real artistic talent in the construction of his store than we ever came in contact with heretofore. It is simply elegant, and we regret we can not speak of its merits in detail. Of Mr. Throne personally. it can be readily understood that he is a man full of enterprise and energy. He is one of the city's leading business men, honored and respected by all who know him. He established his present business in 1877. He is a native of Ohio, coming here from that state in 1872. Being a man of rare executive ability, as well as refined tastes, Mr. Throne has arranged his store into departments exclusive of each other and which for cleanliness and systematic conduct are models which many business men might follow with profit to themselves and comfort to their patrons.

Interior of Henry Throne store

Ottumwa 1890

Myer C. Rice Clothier, 228 E. Main

GEO. W. THOMAS, Photographer, 206 to 212 South Market street. Mr. Thomas is doing a very extensive business in the making of photographs and crayon portraits throughout this and adjoining counties ; in fact he is doing more business in the state than any other photographer. He came here in 1888, and being a young man of exceptionable business ability, enterprise and energy, he soon attracted public attention and public patronage. The quality of his work is attested by the increasing patronage bestowed upon him. His prices are made to meet the condition of the times and can not fail to please all who patronize him. From seven to eight experienced people are constantly employed in the seven large rooms occupied by his studio. Mr. Thomas has spared no expense in fitting up his rooms and claims to have the best equipped ones in the state.

2011 edition

OTTUMWA PRODUCT.   Thomas Photographer.

Ottumwa 1890

B. A. BURDICK, the local manager of the Western Union Telegraph Company's business, is one of the most popular young men in the city, and the editor of this book feels that his work would be unsatisfactory to many Ottumwa people without proper mention of Burdick. He was born in Utica, Wis., in 1862. Mr. Burdick is a graduate of one of the leading business colleges in Wisconsin and eminently fitted for mercantile pursuits. He entered the employ of the Western Union Telegraph Company nine years ago and has been with them continually ever since, arising by steady application and close observance of his employers' interests to his present  position of trust and confidence. He came to Ottumwa about two years ago and has made himself well known and popular to the business community and kept his company on good terms with all customers by his considerate and courteous treatment. Mr. Burdick is married and has two children.

J. H. CHENOWETH, Manufacturer and Dealer in Concrete Pavement and Sidewalks. The process by which Mr. Chenoweth manufactures imitation stone for sidewalks and pavements is a secret of his, which he carefully guards; and that he has occasion for so doing is evidenced by the fact that by and through his process he is enabled to manufacture the finest and most thoroughly satisfactory stone ever produced in the United States. He has no fear of competition, and therefore pays no attention whatever to other manufacturers and dealers, being always sure of every order he solicits or bids for. He will take and fill orders from any part of the United States and guarantee his stone and his work. He has laid thousands of feet of concrete sidewalks in Ottumwa and other cities in the west and south, all of which have received the highest praise and given complete satisfaction. Mr. Chenoweth was born in Paris, France, in 1861, where he learned his trade, coming to America in 1874, and in 1876 began his first work in this line in Des Moines, Iowa.

Communications addressed to him at 228 West Main street.

A. W. THOMA, Retail Jeweler, 115 East Main street. Mr. Thoma is a new star in the mercantile firmament of Ottumwa, but he is a genuine hustler and promises to make it decidedly interesting for his competitors in the jewelry trade in Ottumwa and the surrounding country. He is one of the five brothers engaged in the same business and who by forming a pool in making their purchases from the manufacturers of their goods are able to secure lower figures than are given to dealers giving small orders. He claims, and stands ready to prove it, that he can and will sell watches of every make for less money than any other house in Ottumwa as well as all kinds of jewelry. He makes a specialty of Crystalline glasses at fifty cents per pair. The different stores of this combination of brothers are located as follows—Ottumwa, Iowa; Kalamazoo, Three Rivers, Battle Creek, Mich., and South Bend, Ind. They sell goods at wholesale and retail. A letter to any of these stores will convince all retail dealers that they can buy goods of them cheaper than they can from the factories. Any one in need of a watch or jewelry should call on or write them. Has had the best experience under practical watchmakers. Fine watches and jewelry repaired.

G. W. SOMMERVILLE, Pension Claim Agent, 234 East Main street, came here from Keo Sau Qua,[sic] Iowa, in 1884, where he had resided for twenty-two years. He served three years in Company H, 19th Iowa Volunteer Infantry, entering as 4th Sergeant, graduating to Captain. He has just completed a history of his company, from the time of their enlistment up to the present, and also including a full history of the 19th Iowa Regiment Volunteers. Mr. Sommerville is an easy, graceful and forceful writer, and his work shows literary ability of a superior order. He has woven in many thrilling incidents with the skill of a novelist, thus greatly increasing its attractiveness. A feature of the work will be fine portraits of Maj.-Gen. Herron, Lieut.-Col. McFarland and Capt. Sommerville. Aside from the position of Pension Agent, Capt. Sommerville is resident agent for the Union Pacific Railway Company. He was deputy sheriff of Van Buren county for six years and sheriff for four years.

E. ADAMS HOLT, Insurance, Room 1 Sax Building, Main street. Mr. Holt is the most prominent representative of fire insurance companies in Ottumwa. His companies represent upwards of 100,000,000 capital, and are acknowledged to be as strong and conservative as any engaged in business in the United States. They are as follows : American, of New York; American, of Boston; Girard, of Philadelphia, Pa.; Union and United Firemen, of Philadelphia; Orient, of Hartford, Conn.; Concordia, Northwestern Mutual and Milwaukee Mechanics', of Milwaukee, Wis.; Hawk Eye, of Des Moines, Iowa; German, of Freeport, Ill., and Farmers', of York, Pa. Mr. Holt is a man of sterling qualities of character, than whom none stand higher in the confidence of the people or are more universally respected. His experience in the insurance business extends over a period of twenty-eight years. Although but two years in this state he has already built up a large patronage.

S. E. ADLER, Lawyer and Pension Attorney, 213 Main street. Mr. Adler came here in 1874 and began the practice of his profession. Being an able lawyer and learned man, he soon won distinction and prestige and a large clientage. He practices in all the courts of the country. As a successful pension collector and prosecutor of unallowed claims, he has won a wide reputation. he is a genial, courteous gentleman, whom it is a pleasure to meet.

La Force House, later used as a hospital and as apartments before being demolished

LA FORCE HOUSE, 921 East Main street. This large and commodious hotel occupies a commanding position on the main thoroughfare of the city, overlooking the beautiful Des Moines valley. The electric street cars pass its doors, giving guests rapid transit to all parts of the city. It has one hundred rooms, all of which are large, airy and pleasant. The whole building is heated by steam and lighted by electricity. It is conducted by Mr. John Milburn, one of the best known residents of the city, the former president of a large flouring mill company. The building is owned by Dr. La Force, an able physician and surgeon. His office and drug store is located in the basement, and is conducted by one of his sons, B. D. La Force, a registered pharmacist and graduate of the Illinois State Pharmaceutical College at Chicago.

Ottumwa 1890

POE UNDERWOOD, Druggist, corner of Main and Union streets. Mr. Underwood is one of the few enterprising young men now engaged in business who were born and raised here. After a thorough apprenticeship in the drug business in one of the leading stores in Des Moines he returned to Ottumwa and purchased the stock and good will of the store now occupied by him. He is not only a first-class prescription druggist, but a thorough business man of more than ordinary ability, who will soon rise to a leading place in his profession. He is popular in social and business circles and has legions of friends in this city and also in Des Moines. He keeps a full line of all goods carried by the drug trade. He is doing a successful and rapidly increasing business. The publishers of this book take pleasure in giving his portrait a place in the gallery of representative business men of the city.

F. M. MANGAN, Dealer in Staple and Fancy Groceries, 608 East Main street. Mr. Mangan is one of Ottumwa's most enterprising merchants and a gentleman who merits a place among the business men presented in this book. While attentive to business and conducting a first-class grocery store, he does not forget his duties as a patriotic citizen, and is always ready and eager to do everything possible to assist in advancing the city's interests and bringing her many advantages before the people. Mr. Mangan's genial manners and kind disposition has won for him the confidence and respect of all who know him.

B. BROKENSHAR, Dealer in Hardware, Stoves and Tinware, 103 South Court street. Mr. Brokenshar is one of Ottumwa's self-made business men. He came here from England in 1882 and immediately accepted an humble position in the pork-packing house of Morrell & Co., where he served six years. In 1888 he severed his connection with the company to enter business for himself, and opened a hardware and second-hand store. It will not be amiss to mention the fact that he carries the only wholesale stock of stove repairs in the city. He always keeps on hand a large assortment of second-hand hardware and furniture goods and is in the market to buy or sell at all times.

GOTTLIEB BECK, Bakery, Confectionery and Cigar Dealer, 106 South Market street. Mr. Beck is one of Ottumwa's foremost and leading business men. he came here in 1881 and for three years was connected with the bakery firm of Lowenberg Bros. In 1884 he opened his present large establishment and from that time up to the present he has enjoyed a large and continuously increasing patronage. Having had twenty years' experience in the business, he is able to turn out as fine goods as any concern in the country. Mr. Beck is a native of New Jersey, going from there to St. Louis, where he spent five years in his profession. He employs a large force of experienced help and can always fill orders by mail promptly on time. Mr. Beck is a man of excellent business ability, energy and enterprise, always ready to extend generous aid to any and all projects that will add to the city's growth and prosperity.

2. Gottlieb Beck.

F. SILBERMAN & Bros., Wholesale Dealers in Hides and Wool, 124 East Second street. Main house, 212 and 214 Michigan street, Chicago. This is one of the wealthiest and largest wool and hide firms in the United States, and perhaps in the world. Three floors in the large building they occupy here, are constantly being filled and emptied with wool and hides. While this branch shipped over 800,000 pounds of wool since June 1, 1890, it is but a small proportion of the business done by the home house in Chicago. This house alone ships about 1,000,000 pounds of wool in a season. Since June 1st the firm have handled, altogether, over 4,000,000 pounds of domestic wool. This branch shipped twenty-five car loads of hides during July and August, and these are the dullest months of the year in the hide business. The firm is composed of three brothers, F., S., and A. Silberman. They have a branch store in Quincy, Ill., where they first engaged in the business in 1866. Each member of the firm has had twenty-six years' experience in the business, and consequently no better judges of wool and hides can be found. Mr. A. Silberman, the resident partner, is much respected by the citizens of Ottumwa, where he has made many warm friends in social and business circles.

Ottumwa 1890

ERNEST KOCH, Architect, corner of Court and Second streets. It can truthfully be said of Mr. Koch that he is one of the leading architects of this country. Not satisfied with all the learning gained from the architectural schools in this country he visited Germany, spending four years in one of the architectural colleges there and from which he graduated with the highest honors. Upon his return from Germany he located at Wheeling, W. Va., where he practiced his profession for six years with splended [sic] success. He came to Ottumwa in 1880 and has resided here continously [sic] since that time. Evidences of his superiority as an artist and architect are shown in many beautiful residences in the city, among which may be mentioned those of Messrs. Allmayer, Ray, Foster, Evans, Harper, Peters and others, together with an imposing church edifice at Sigourney, Iowa, Normal School building at Hettich [sic], Iowa, and many smaller structures. Mr. Koch earnestly solicits correspondence from people desiring to build.

J. M. WINN, Photographer, 209 and 211 East Main street. Mr. Winn is not only a first-class photographer but a wholesouled, genial gentleman, whom everybody likes and respects. He spent four years in the Union army as scout and dispatch bearer, one of the most hazardous and responsible positions which a soldier is called upon to fill. He remained in the ranks to the close of the war, when he received an honorable discharge from service. As a photographer and business man Mr. Winn's success is phenomenal—quite equal to his success as a scout and soldier. For twenty years he has been engaged in this business, and during this time he has built up a reputation and patronage second to none in the country.

J. C. RANSEEN, Tailor, 305 East Main street. Mr. Ranseen is one of the few really first-class tailors engaged in the profession; one of the few who can guarantee a fit equal to those of the best tailors in Chicago or New York, and in the very latest styles. Mr. Ranseen has had twenty years' experience in the business and does his own cutting and fitting. With the system employed by him for self-measurement, he makes suits for customers out of town that fit equally as well as those made from measurements taken by himself. He sends samples through the mail to out-of-town customers and instructions for self-measurement. Always affable and pleasant, Mr. Ranseen makes friends quickly and they remember  him as a business man who has done his best to please them. We advise those who read this notice, and who cannot call at Mr. Ranseen's store, to send to him for samples and prices, satisfied that he can make you a suit that will please you and for less money than any former suit cost not purchased of him. He keeps ten thoroughly experienced tailors and can fill any order given him on the very shortest notice.

E. GINN, Grocery and Fruits, 108 East Main street. Mr. Ginn is one of the enterprising young merchants engaged in business in Ottumwa that have by careful industry and energy pushed their way upward to success and a leading position in the mercantile world. He opened his grocery store in 1882 in the face of strong competition and with many misgivings as to the future, but determined to win patronage and public favor if honorable treatment and square dealing could accomplish it. That he has succeeded is shown by the fact that he numbers many of the leading people of the city among his customers. The stock carried by Mr. Ginn is a very choice and complete one.

Ottumwa 1890

W. M. RIDEOUT, General Cooperage and Wholesale Shipper of Poultry, Mill street, between College and Union streets. Mr. Rideout has the satisfaction of knowing that he is at the head of the largest cooperage factory in Iowa and perhaps in the entire West. The factory was built by H. W. Moses in 1874, and was operated by him up to 1878, when Mr. Rideout purchased it. He employs forty experienced coopers and helpers, who turn out 70,000 butter tubs and firkins every year, aside from a large amount of custom work. One traveling salesman is kept on the road continuously visiting the principal shipping points in Iowa, Missouri and Kansas. The best butter tubs and firkins made in the state, or United States, come from this factory, every one of which is made from the most carefully selected lumber. The tubs are made of white ash and the firkins of white oak, all of which is shipped here from Wisconsin, Michigan and Indiana. Mr. Rideout guarantees all his work, an absolute safeguard against an inferior article. Some idea of the magnitude of this gentleman's business may be gained from his sales of tubs and firkins to one firm last year, that of Baker Bros., in the sum of $15,000. In the poultry trade he also does an enormous business, as can readily be understood from the fact that in three months he has paid out $14,000 in purchase money alone. In 1889 he shipped sixty tons of poultry, a figure that will be largely exceeded in 1890. At Carson, Iowa, he has a branch house giving employment to fifteen hands, and doing a business proportionately as large as the one here. Mr. Rideout is one of the leading, foremost business men and manufacturers of Ottumwa, a man who stands second to none in the respect and confidence of the people. In business, straightforward and honorable, in private life gentlemanly, reserved and generous. In all matters pertaining to the welfare and advancement of the city he is always relied upon to give liberally.

8. W. M. Rideout.

E. H. MATHER & BRO., Plumbers and Gas Fitters. Conscientiousness, more than ordinary intelligence and a thorough acquaintance with the laws of sanitary science are requisites more necessary in the plumbers profession than in any other. If people were aware of the number of deaths caused by defective work in the plumbing of houses, there would certainly be a very large number of so-called plumbers out of work in a very short time. Edward H. and Chas. B. Mather are leaders in their profession, painstaking, careful men, who are always ready to guarantee every job they undertake, men who make a study of sanitary science and adopt the latest and best improved methods for making plumbing in a house safe and reliable and not a death-dealing agent—a monster of destructiveness. Their aim is to lead, and that they succeed is demonstrated by the fact that they secure the contracts for doing all the plumbing and gas fitting in the finest public and private buildings and residences in the city as well as large numbers of them in different portions of the state. They employ a force of the most thoroughly experienced workmen in the country and are enabled to do the largest jobs in the shortest possible time. Ed. Mather is a member of the Masonic lodge here, and C. B. is a member of the Knights of Pythias.

CLAUDE M. MYERS, Retail Confectioner, Dealer in Fruits, Cigars, etc., 110 East Second street. In making a record of the leading merchants of the city there are many who are deserving of more space than others by reason of their great enterprise, energy and activity, and which we would gladly accord them if possible. Among this class Mr. Myers is worthy of special mention. He is one of the few business men that fully appreciate and understand that to secure public patronage one must merit it. He realizes that the merchant of to-day must not only keep abreast of the times but in advance of them—in other words lead all competitors. This is the secret of Mr. Myers' success. In July, 1889, he opened his present store and ice cream parlors, which he spared no expense in fitting up in metropolitan style, and stocking it with the finest and freshest goods in the market, to which he added lines not carried by other dealers, yet always in public favor and demand. This. was enterprise that he knew would win, and it did. He made a bid for patronage and got it, and is now as thoroughly energetic in striving to increase it—and he'll do it.

Ottumwa 1890

J. W. CALHOUN, 306 East Main street, in the Ballingall Hotel, enjoys the reputation of being the leading dealer in Hats and Men's Furnishing Goods in the city. The business was originally started by L. Williams in 1882, and was purchased by Mr. Calhoun Sept. 14, 1885. The store is elegantly fitted up and the freshest of each season's novelties is temptingly displayed. Previous to Mr. Calhoun's assuming the reins of the business the trade was strictly confined to Ottumwa. Mr. Calhoun is now represented on the road in all the principal towns of southern Iowa and northern Missouri. As a result of regular visits to these points a large trade has sprung up and Mr. Calhoun is known for many miles around as well as in Ottumwa where he enjoys the patronage and esteem of the best element. His specialty is shirts and suitings made to measure, his stock is the most complete in its line, and the best citizens have learned to regard him as a criterion for the prevailing styles. He is agent for the celebrated Dunlap hat, which is recognized by devotees of fashion as the leader in style and quality.

J.W. Calhoun, standing in the doorway of his store

J. W. GARNER, Wholesale Dry Goods and Notions. This wholesale house is one of the largest and most successful outside of Chicago in the entire Northwest. The store is located at Nos. 108 to 116 Market street, and from basement to roof is filled with one of the finest and most complete stocks of dry goods and notions possible to find in any house in the country. Mr. Garner established himself in the wholesale business here in 1867, and has remained in the harness and in active control of it up to the present with excellent prospects of many more years of equal activity. The mammoth business done by this house to-day bears no resemblance whatever to the modest one conducted by Mr. Garner twenty-three years ago. Then a few local merchants in this and neighboring towns were supplied by him; to-day he counts his customers by the hundreds in as many towns all over this Western country. This splendid success is

3. J. W. Garner.

indebted to something more than business ability, for it is an age when all sorts of methods are employed to secure trade. To those who know Mr. Garner the secret of his success is understood, and carries with it respect and admiration. To always sell goods upon their merits and never misrepresent them in any way is what will gain and retain the respect and confidence of retail merchants and hold their trade against all competitors. This notice would not be complete without mentioning Mr. Garner's patriotism to Ottumwa and his pride in its growth and prosperity. There are none more liberal than he in contributing to any and all enterprises which have for their object the advancement of the city's interests. Some idea of his importance as a potent factor in the city's growth may be realized from the mention of some of the enterprises he is connected with. He is a director in the Ottumwa Savings Bank; vice-president of the Ottumwa Electric Light, Steam Heating and Railway Company; a director of the Wapello County Fair Association; vice-president of the Ottumwa Opera House Company, and a member of the executive committee of the Ottumwa Coal Palace Association. A cut of Mr. Garner's beautiful residence, on East Second street, is shown on another page, as is also an excellent photograph of himself.

Ottumwa 1890

J. A. MANGAN, Real Estate, 213 East Main street. The prosperity of a city depends more largely upon its reputable real estate dealers than the average citizen realizes. The real estate dealer is the ideal American hustler, to whom can be credited the securing of more enterprises for his city than to any other business or profession. The development of the natural resources of the city and surrounding country and increase in manufacturing concerns, etc., are of more concern to the real estate man than to any other citizen, for they are things necessary to his. continuance in business ; their increase and development mean the advancement of prices and the demand for real estate. Mr. Mangan is one of the thoroughly reliable and responsible men engaged in the business here who tend to elevate it. He is a firm believer in Ottumwa's future greatness, but he is buying and selling realty on the basis of values which the city's present development and condition justifies. Ottumwa is coming to the front with longer and more rapid strides than ever she has taken in the past, and real estate, to keep pace with her, must advance over present prices very materially and rapidly. To invest in city property to-day is the safest and most remunerative one possible to make anywhere in the United States. Write to Mr. Mangan and get a list of his offerings and prices. Any statement he may make can be fully relied upon as the absolute truth.

5. J. A. Mangan.

E. J. MCLAUGHLIN, Wholesale and Retail Groceries, Teas and Coffees, 310 East Main street. E. J. McLaughlin is one of Ottumwa's great wholesale merchants. For twenty years he has been shipping his goods throughout this and adjoining states, and for twenty years he has been adding customer after customer to his long list, and every one of them his friend—first a customer, soon a friend. Mr. McLaughlin is personally very popular. but it is through his popular, manly business methods and the sale of superior goods (which always reach their destination exactly as ordered) that he relies for patronage. He has been in the tea business for thirty-five years, and is to-day the best judge of tea in the west. He has been in the grocery, tea and coffee business combined for twenty years. His specialties are tea, tobacco and roasted coffee; all roasted coffee sold by him is roasted under his direct supervision in his large wholesale house. Two traveling salesmen are out on the road continuously, while a large force of help is kept busy in the stores, filling orders for shipment and waiting upon customers in the retail department. Mr. McLaughlin claims that he can sell the same quality of goods as cheap, if not cheaper, than any other house in the west, Chicago not excepted, and all he asks is a chance to prove it. Of Mr. McLaughlin personally nothing further need be said than that no man in Ottumwa is more popular or held in greater respect than he.

Federal Building / Post Office under construction (completed 1889)

Ottumwa 1890

FRED ROSEN & BRO. Retail Dry Goods, Carpets, Boots and Shoes, 202 East Main street. This firm is one of the leading retail business houses of the city. They carry a very large stock, complete in every branch and replete with the latest styles and novelties of the seasons. The firm was organized in 1884, buying out the business of Geo. H. Sheffer. By catering to the demands of the public and conducting their business on honorable and straightforward principles and backed by one of the finest stocks of goods in the city they have gained the confidence and esteem of a large number of patrons.

Fred Rosen was born January 10, 1843, in Falkoping, Sweden. At a very early age he lost both parents and was thrown upon his own resources in the world. For nine years he worked on a farm. In 1868 he was married to Miss Kate Lindburg, of his own town. In the spring of 1869 he sailed for America with his wife and brother William, coming direct to Ottumwa, through the advice of a half-brother in Mt. Pleasant. When he arrived he had but three dollars to his name. For three months he worked on a farm, then followed over two years of section labor on the C. B. & Q. Ry., during the winter time sawing wood for parties in Ottumwa. It is hardly credible that this prosperous merchant of to-day so short a time ago was seen going through alleyways with his sawbuck on his shoulder. Following this he worked as car inspector on the Rock Island road for twelve years, until he joined his brother in the dry goods business. Mr. Rosen's reward for perseverance and hard work is shown in four splendid pieces of improved residence property, his present business and a very snug bank account. Above all he has a large family consisting of three girls and two boys. The oldest of the children, Miss Emma, has been book-keeper and cashier in the store for the past five years. She has a thorough business education and is an indispensable help in the store.

2011 edition

WILLIAM ROSEN was born May 26, 1849, in Falkoping, Sweden. Upon the death of his surviving parent, his mother, when he was sixteen years old, he went to Stockholm and attended business college for two years. From there he entered a normal school at Gothenburg, where he studied two years more, and then came to this country with his brother. At first he found employment at farming, afterwards working at the C. B. & Q. roundhouse until 1874, when he secured a position as house salesman in Stewart's music store, leaving there in 1876 to clerk in Jordan & Sons' dry goods house. In 1880 he entered the employ of Geo. H. Sheffer, and four years later with his brother bought out his employer. He was married in 1880 to Matilda C. Johnson, also a native of Sweden. They have been blessed with two children, a boy and girl, the latter having died. Both he and his brother are prominent members and officers of the Swedish Lutheran church.

Workers on the chocolates manufacturing line at Hall Candy Company

Ottumwa 1890

1. Sam'l Loeb.

SAMUEL LOEB, Cigar Manufacturer and Retail Dealer in fine cigars, tobacco and smokers' supplies, is located in large and splendidly equipped rooms at No. 215 East Main street. Mr. Loeb is one of the most thoroughly enterprising young business men in Ottumwa, and is deserving of great credit for the success he has attained in the manufacture of fine cigars. He was formerly in his father's employ in the cigar store located in the Ballingall house, and altogether has had thirteen years' experience in the business. In 1888 he conceived the idea of starting a cigar factory "on his own hook," notwithstanding the fact that the competition among local as well as foreign dealers was very strong in Ottumwa, and immediately took steps for the establishment of himself in the business. The result has proved the wisdom of his judgment. He now employs seven experienced cigar-makers and will soon increase that number and enlarge his present quarters or move to more commodious ones. Some idea of his success can be realized by the fact that the entire product of his factory is consumed in this city. He is the maker of the famous "Sam'l of Posen" and "Resolution" cigars, the sale of which has never been equaled by any other cigar manufactured here.

J. P. ULLRICH, Manufacturer of Wagons and Carriages, Dealer in and Manufacturer of Mining Tools and Machinery, 219 South Jefferson street. Mr. Ullrich makes the most substantial wagons and carriages to be found in this or any other state. He does nearly all his work by hand, and as he uses none but the very best and most thoroughly seasoned timber, he can always guarantee every wagon or carriage which leaves his shops. In the wood-work department he has one of the most skilled and experienced workmen, Mr. John McCue. For thirty years Mr. McCue has devoted his undivided time and attention to this work, and as a consequence, he stands to-day in the very front ranks of expert wagon and carriage makers in this country. Mr. Ullrich came here from Centerville, Iowa, where he was engaged in the same business, and entered the Woolen Mills Company, of which he remained a member up to 1890, when he opened this present factory.

FRED W. WILSON, Wholesale Dealer in Fruits, Vegetables, Oysters, etc., 404 and 406 E. Main street. This is one of the oldest and largest fruit and commission houses in Iowa. The business was started in 1870 by W. R. Daum, in a small way, and increased from year to year. In 1888 Mr. Wilson purchased the entire business and has conducted it since with the greatest success. He is a Philadelphian by birth, and came here in 1878. He was for ten years, cashier and assistant manager with the famous Ottumwa packing firm, Jno. Morrell & Co., Limited. By strict attention to every detail of his business, Mr. Wilson has built it up until the receipts average from $75,000 to $100,000 per year, extending over a territory covering southern Iowa and northern Missouri. He purchases fruits direct from the growers in California and Florida, and foreign fruits from importers in New York and New Orleans. In the winter season his oyster trade is a special feature, purchasing direct from the packers in Baltimore. In the spring and early summer he ships large quantities of small fruits and vegetables from the gardens in Arkansas, Missouri and Louisiana. Mr. Wilson is counted among our youngest and most successful business men. His beautiful home on East Fourth street is shown among the illustrations.

J. T. Hackworth home - Southeast corner of N. Court & Pennsylvania.

Ottumwa 1890

E. L. LATHROP, Physician and Surgeon, 222 East Main street. Dr. Lathrop enjoys one of the finest medical and surgical practices in the West. As a surgeon he stands pre-eminently first in the state. he is from Madison county, New York; was assistant surgeon of the Tenth Illinois Cavalry; is a graduate of Rush Medical College, where the Museum of Comparative Anatomy owes its existence to him. He practiced in Chicago from 1866 to 1870, previous to coming here. As a geologist he is one of the most enthusiastic in the country. His private collection, most of which has been donated by him to the Smithsonian Institution, at Washington, was the largest in the state. He succeeded in getting up one of the very finest features in the Coal Palace exhibit, consisting of nearly 6,000 specimens of Geology, donated by 101 different residents of counties near by. The exhibit represented relics of the Indians, a very complete fossil collection of bones, shells, coal, sandstone and limestone, and curios from all over the world. This was a feature of the Coal Palace that attracted larger crowds than any other, and was visited by many students of natural history from all over the country. The Doctor devoted a great deal of time and expense to this work, and the many words of praise elicited from visitors were richly merited by him.

It is the intention of the Coal Palace directory to have a much larger exhibit next year, and circulars will be mailed residents of Iowa, asking their aid for the project in the early spring. For some years most of the fine animals which have died in Forepaugh's and in Cole's circuses have been sent to Dr. Lathrop, to be prepared by him for his private museum. The collection includes snakes, tigers, lions, varieties of foreign deer, seal, zebra and other animals.

O. E. STEWART, Division Superintendent, East Iowa Division Chicago, Burlington & Quincy Railway, has headquarters in this city. He is a native of this state, born in Henry county, in 1868. At the age of seventeen he entered the army and served four years in Co. E, 15th Iowa Infantry, and is Past Post Commander of Matthies Post No. 5, at Burlington. Mr. Stewart is a thorough railroad man. Starting in when very young as station agent at Danville, Iowa, he has been promoted since to many positions, including that of Ticket Agent at Omaha, Council Bluffs, Red Oak and other points, Train Dispatcher, Train Master, Superintendent of Telegraph, Assistant Superintendent and then Division Superintendent in July, 1889, the position he now fills. By his kind and considerate treatment and attentive business methods he has become one of the most popular and valuable railroad men on the line.

COAL COMPANIES.

PHILLIPS FUEL COMPANY. The mining of coal is the principal industry of Iowa next to that of farming, as will be seen by reference to the statistics presented on another page. One of the leading companies engaged in this business is the Phillips Fuel Company, with headquarters at 105 Court street. Their mines are located at points varying from two to forty miles from the city. They employ about six hundred hands, and mine from seven to eight hundred tons of coal per day. The coal from their mines is adapted to both steam and domestic purposes, their mines at Mystic and Brazil yielding an especially superior article for heating and cooking, while that at Ottumwa and Willard equals any coal in the West for steam uses. It finds a ready market all over Iowa, Nebraska, Minnesota, and the Dakotas. The officers of the company are as follows : Ira Phillips, president; B. A. Cleveland, vice-president; Henry Phillips, secretary, and E. L. Kilby, treasurer. Authorized capital stock, $500,000; $200,000 paid in. Their offices are at 105 Court street.

Phillips Coal Company mine

Ottumwa 1890

THE SOAP CREEK COAL COMPANY is one of the wealthy coal companies operating in Iowa, whose headquarters are in Ottumwa. This company has a capital of $200,000, employs 200 men, and mines upwards of 300 tons of coal per day. Their mines are located at Foster, Iowa. The coal from these mines is an Al steam coal and is the preference of locomotive engineers because of its heat-giving qualities, freedom from clinkers, easy combustion and, lasting qualities in the furnace. It is also largely used for domestic purposes. The coal from this company's mines is shipped to all parts of Iowa, Minnesota and the Dakotas. The officers of the company are as follows: E. I. Foster, of Cedar Rapids, president; Ira Phillips, vice-president, and Henry Phillips, secretary and treasurer. Their offices are located at 105 Court street.

THE OTTUMWA FUEL COMPANY, located at 430 East Samantha street, is worthy of special mention in the pages of this book. Mrs. Kate M. Ladd is the able president of the company and H. M. Hedrick is its secretary and treasurer. The business was started by B. W. Ladd, in 1875, who was succeeded by Chas. F. C. Ladd and J. A. Sunderland, and conducted by them until the death of Chas. F. C. Ladd eight years ago, at which time the present company was started and Mrs. Ladd, the widow of Chas. F. C. Ladd, became president and Mr. Hedrick became secretary and treasurer. The company is very popular with the people and are [sic] doing one of the largest retail trades of the city. They handle the finest coal produced in Iowa, together with anthracite from Pennsylvania. Their yards and sheds are the most extensive in the city. In fine coal for blacksmiths' use they have a large trade, making this a special feature of their business. They have contracted with the Whitebreast Fuel Company for the exclusive sale of the coal from their new mine recently opened, and in order to handle their large trade in the west end of the city have opened a branch yard on South Benton street.
Mr. Hedrick is well known to the citizens of Ottumwa and southern Iowa as an honorable, upright young man of excellent business ability, who enjoys the confidence and respect of all who know him. He is a son of the late Gen. J. M. Hedrick.

2. Appanoose Coal Co., R. D. Rosser, Supt.   3. Appanoose Coal Co., Store and Dwellings.

APPANOOSE COAL & FUEL COMPANY, Ottumwa, Iowa. This is one of the most successful and best conducted companies in the state. The capital stock is $100,000. The officers are highly respected business men of unimpeachable character and splendid executive ability. W. J. Burnett is president; E. E. McElroy, vice-president; F. B. Cresswell, secretary, and Richard Rosser, superintendent. The company employ seventy-five miners, and ship fifteen to twenty cars and upwards of coal per day to points in Minnesota, North and South Dakota and Iowa. Experts pronounce the coal mined by this company the best in Iowa. It is, they say, remarkably clean, there being nothing in it that does not burn up, leaving no clinkers and a clear white ash, while its lasting and heat-giving qualities are unequaled. The mines are located ten miles southwest of Ottumwa on the C. M. & St. P. R. R. The vein is very regular, averaging about four feet without "breaks" or "faults," and with an exceptionally fine roof. The shaft is dry and clean, a circumstance of importance in coal mining. Any one desiring to invest in mines, mining stock, or coal lands should write this company. The property extends over 400 acres at Appanoose, and the company owns and has control of 500 acres in Appanoose county near Darby on the C. M. & St. P. Ry.

Ottumwa 1890

THE HAWKEYE COAL AND MINING COMPANY, with head offices at 112 South Market street, is one of the corporations located here that are doing much to advance the city's interests and further develop the great industry of coal mining. Their extensive mines are located two and one-half miles north of the city in Wapello county, on the line of the C. M. & St. Paul railroad, where they have a large force of men employed. The coal from this company's mines is of a very superior quality and finds ready sale in competition with Illinois coal as well as coal from other states. This company was organized and begun [sic] business in 1886. The officers of the company are well known and highly respected citizens of Ottumwa. They are: A. C. Caughlan, president; F. S. Warder, vice-president; J. R. Burgess, secretary, and E. D. Fair, treasurer. The company owns and controls large tracts of valuable coal lands, most of which they expect to develop. They also buy and sell coal lands, and anyone wishing to invest in this class of security should write to them for information relative to the lands still in the market.

T. E. MUIR, conducts one of the largest wholesale and retail trades in fuel of all kinds in the city. He handles and keeps in stock everything in the fuel line and gives employment to twenty men. Mr. Muir is one of Ottumwa's most prominent citizens, having lived and been in business here since 1867. He first entered the grocery business; in which he remained two years, leaving it to go into the freight and transfer business, in which he engaged for eight years; afterwards went into the ice business for a period of seven years, and in 1884 into the fuel business. Mr. Muir is a successful business man, never failing to make any enterprise in which he engages return him fair remuneration. He has ability as a manager and financier, and he never fails to make friends of his customers and associates, and as a consequence, he is one of the most popular men in Ottumwa. In the fuel business he can fill an order for Iowa or Pennsylvania coal for less money than is ordinarily paid for the same article and guarantee full weight and equal quality. His yards and sheds are very extensive and his facilities for prompt filling of orders can not be excelled. Mr. Muir's portrait appears on another page.

6. T. E. Muir.

Ottumwa 1890

CHARLES SCHICK is one of the leading manufacturers of Iowa, and one of her most highly respected citizens. His large stave and barrel factory, run in connection with a large saw-mill, is among the largest industries of Ottumwa. He also owns a half interest in the Schick & Pratt brick-yards located here which turn out one million and upwards of brick annually The firm have facilities for making all kinds of brick and for filling all orders for common inside to fine pressed and fire brick in the shortest possible space of time. A new discovery of an excellent quality of clay for paving-brick, places this firm in the lead of all others on this article. Aside from the brick-yard, stave-factory, saw-mill, barrel factory and lumber yard, Mr. Schick owns and looks after several large apartment houses and a large stock and dairy farm adjoining the city on the north. It can be readily understood that Mr. Schick is a very wealthy man and a man of superior business capacity and great executive ability. He was born in Hesse Darmstadt, Germany, July 24, 1847. He came to America at the age of two years with his parents, and after living in the states of New York, Wisconsin, Iowa and Kansas, he went at an early age to California with his father. They located at Santa Clara, where Mr. Schick attended the University of The Pacific for two years, removed to San Jose and engaged in the manufacture of brick with his father until 1866 when he moved to Davenport, Iowa, where he engaged in farming for three years, coming to Ottumwa in 1869 to establish his mills and brick-yards.

2011 edition

HON. E. L. BURTON is one of Iowa's most learned and able lawyers and one of her most honored representative citizens. He is recognized by all members of his profession as one of the most fair-minded and able jurists in the West, one whose rulings are rarely ever questioned and as rarely reversed by the Supreme Court. A gifted, eloquent speaker, his pleas to the bench or jury were always sure to bring together a crowd of brother lawyers. Possessed of an analytical mind he reaches below the surface to bring forth motives which would pass unnoticed by less acute intellects. Perhaps that which impresses one most in listening to his rulings or to one of his pleas for a client, is his sincerity. To him sophistry is an unknown quantity. In his official position he is dignified and stern, yet beneath it all the light of a warm heart and pleasant disposition can always be seen. More could be said of one of Ottumwa's most distinguished citizens, Judge Burton, but it always proves a difficult task to speak of people as we feel they deserve until they have passed beyond the reach of our voices, simply because we respect that modesty so grandly characteristic of American citizens. Judge Burton came to this city from New York in 1855, and practiced law until 1878, when he was elected Judge of the Second Judicial District, the position he now holds and which he occupied continuously up to 1886, leaving it to go back to his practice in which he continued up to 1890, being then appointed Judge of this district to fill an unexpired term. He was nominated on the Democratic ticket this fall to continue in the office for which he is so eminently qualified.

4. Judge E. L. Burton.

Judge E. L. Burton home -
South Elm Street,
north of Lincoln Avenue

Ottumwa 1890

FRANK MYERS, Saddlery and Harness, 102 Court street. Mr. Myers is one of Ottumwa's self-made business men, born and raised here. He learned his trade in Agency City, and has been in active business for himself for nearly seven years. He makes a specialty of fine harness and saddles, and his goods in these lines can not be excelled by any manufactured here or elsewhere. He likes his profession or trade, and delights in devoting himself in special efforts to turning out the finest goods possible to create. He keeps a large stock of everything in the horse furnishing goods line, and at
prices that can not be lowered, quality and workmanship considered. Mr. Myers willingly guarantees every article leaving his factory, and to those who know him his guarantee is a positive safeguard against loss—he is an honest, upright business man, enjoying the full confidence of all who know him. He keeps five thoroughly experienced men employed, and his trade reaches out over this and many adjoining counties. Write to him for prices.

W. C. WYMAN, member of the Wholesale and Retail Crockery firm of J. Prugh & Co., is one of the leading citizens of Ottumwa, a popular member of society and a splendid business man. He enjoys the comforts of one of the handsomest residences in the city, located on North Court street and overlooking the beautiful Des Moines valley, a cut of which appears on another page.

CLARK, ODENWALDER & Co., Retail Lumber Dealers, located at West Second street, do an immense business in their line, being second to no firm in the city or county in the retail trade. They established the yards in 1885. The firm is represented here by Messrs. August and Charles Odenwalder. Mr. August Odenwalder came here from Wausau, Wis., where he was in the wholesale lumber business three years. The firm have done a large business since entering the field, but are capable of handling much more, and to secure orders from all parts of the state and West they invite all dealers and builders to give them an opportunity to figure on bills before making purchases. Their connections with the largest mills in Wisconsin are such as to enable them to give very low prices on all grades of lumber. They guarantee satisfaction in every instance and being reliable, responsible men, their guaranty is ample protection to the buyer. They carry a heavy stock in their yards here, but in filling the heavy outside orders, they have the lumber shipped directly from their mills in Wisconsin.

8. Chas. Odenwalder.

5. August Odenwalder.

J. A. FREY, Dentist, office corner of Main and Court streets has been practicing here about three years, and enjoys a large and rapidly increasing patronage.

Ottumwa 1890

THE R. T. DAVIS MILL COMPANY, organized in 1867, is one of the largest and most conspicuous concerns engaged in the manufacture of wheat flour in the United States. What is termed as the "Mother House" is located at St. Joseph, Mo., with children (branches) located at Omaha, Nebraska; Des Moines and Ottumwa, Iowa. The officers, all residents of St. Joseph, are as follows: R. T. Davis, president; R. M. Davis, secretary; and J. M. Wilson, Wm. Sallee and R. T. Davis, directors; the last named gentleman being the founder of the company, and its "main-spring" and executive head.

They employ from one hundred and fifty to two hundred hands, and ten traveling salesmen. The capacity of the St. Joseph mills is one thousand barrels per day. They acknowledge no superior, and claim to make the best flour ever placed upon the market, a claim substantiated by many first prize medals from fairs, expositions, etc. At the Iowa State fair of 1889 and 1890 their flour received first premium each year. Their

THE R. T. DAVIS MILL COMPANY.

special brands are: Davis' Royal Patent No. 10, being their standard brand and leader; Davis No. 1, Blue D, Cream Patent. Red F, Golden Sheaf, Hawkeye and Lion. Their mills are equipped with all the modern and latest improved machinery known to the trade. They were designed and built especially for the manufacture of the finest grade of flour possible, and they are steadfastly adhering to the original idea. Mr. G. F. Comegys is the manager of the Ottumwa branch, and a more competent and experienced man could not have been found by the company. He is not only maintaining the reputation of the

G. F. Comegys

company's flour but is bringing trade and making friends by his pleasant, gentlemanly manners, and straightforward, business methods.

EVANS JONES, Master Mechanic of the C. B. & Q. railway, is one of Ottumwa's most respected citizens. The editor takes pleasure in presenting a short biographical sketch of Mr. Jones as an example of a self-made man. How, starting at the lowest round of the ladder in his chosen vocation and working by degrees of pluck and perseverance, adhering strictly and tenaciously to independent principles mapped out for himself, he attained an office of leadership—the fondest hope of the progressive mechanic. Mr. Jones was born in England, June 21, 1845—touched the shores of America with his parents at the age of six. His father located at Utica, N. Y., and conducted a large tannery there for years. The first experience of the subject of this sketch in railroad work was in August, 1864, when he entered the employ of the B. & M. railway shops at Burlington, Iowa, as apprentice. He remained there until 1868, when he left them to go to the Toledo, Peoria & Warsaw

4. Evan Jones.

Company, with headquarters at Peoria. Still working at his trade, he came to Ottumwa in 1870, and entered the employ of the C. B. & Q. railway. His progress was prompt and he advanced with rapidity through the several stages of promotion to his present position, which was conferred upon him in 1880. This is the plain story of an honest mechanic's reward and it should be an encouragement to the many struggling for recognition of their merits. Mr. Jones lives in a handsome residence and has a family of six children, one of which, a daughter, is married.

Ottumwa 1890

JOE N. LAWRENCE, 318 North Green street, is Ottumwa's leading florist. His green-houses are the largest and finest in the state and contain more rare plants and flowers than those of all the other florists of Ottumwa combined. The business was established by Mr. Lawrence in 1870. In furnishing cut flowers for funerals, parties and weddings he is acknowledged to excel all other florists in the state. He fills orders from all parts of the state and, when requested, goes personally to arrange displays. Mr. Lawrence is an enterprising man; in 1870 he began this business in a little green-house ten by thirty, today he has four mammoth houses filled to overflowing. He has one large greenhouse filled with nothing but carnation pinks while another is filled with nothing but smilax. In the spring he raises thousands of bedding plants for residents of the city and state, and in this is considered more successful than any other florist.

OTTUMWA STAMP WORKS AND JOB PRINTING HOUSE, 217 East Main street. This is the largest stamp manufactory west of Chicago. Any thing in the way of rubber stamps from a name stamp to the largest printing wheel and seals of all sizes and descriptions are turned out by this house in a style and finish equal to any manufactured in Chicago or New York; in fact, no finer work is possible in this line of goods. They also carry a very extensive and complete stock of imported stamps, novelties and office supplies. Mr. A. G. Wallace is at the head of this large concern. He is an expert in his trade, having been engaged in it for many years. His goods have a reputation extending over many states and territories and from which he is constantly receiving orders. He also manufactures self-inking printing wheels, carries a very large line of the finest business, calling and wedding cards besides conducting an extensive job printing establishment.

In the matter of fine printing, the work turned out by his presses can not be excelled by the largest printing houses in the United States. Mr. Wallace is a young man full of energy and enterprise, who stands high in the esteem of all who know him.

2011 edition

DR. ALICE M. STARK, Physician and Surgeon, located at 107 North Court street, is Ottumwa's only lady physician. She graduated from Ann Arbor in 1879 and, after practicing in the Boston hospital for one year, came to Ottumwa, where she has since lived and practiced her profession. Miss Stark is recognized as an able physician, and that the people have confidence in her is shown by the fact that she has more than she can do.

C. W. FUNK, Retail Grocer, corner Benton and Sherman streets. Mr. Funk is one of the really live and enterprising merchants of Ottumwa. He came here from Eldon, Iowa, in 1888, and after one year's service as clerk he opened his present store. Mr. Funk enjoys the distinction of being the youngest man in Iowa conducting a mercantile establishment alone and unaided—he is eighteen years of age. His store is filled with one of the choicest and most attractive stocks of groceries to be found in Iowa. He aims to carry everything known to the trade, and to please each and every customer by his careful attention to their wants.

JOHN MULDOON, at 219 East Main street, opened this September one of the finest and largest stocks of queensware to be found in the state. Mr. Muldoon is a native of New York State, but has been in the chinaware business in Harlan and Mt. Pleasant during the past ten years—two years in the latter place. Recognizing the fine opportunity here for such a business as his, he decided to locate permanently, and has placed before the public a choice line of china goods of all kinds, from the plainest to the fanciest variety, and everything pertaining to the queensware business. He has one of the finest Christmas and holiday stocks to be found anywhere. Mr. Muldoon has had years of experience in his line, and he proposes, by honest, legitimate means, to obtain a share of the public patronage. Ottumwa has room for many more such men as Mr. Muldoon, whose enterprising spirit and courteous kindly treatment of all will make him one of Ottumwa's most popular citizens.

Ottumwa 1890

L. M. GODLEY, Deputy Postmaster, is one of the prominent men of the city who deserves mention in this book. Mr. Godley is one of the earliest settlers in the county; was born June 13, 1836; has lived here since he was fourteen years of age; learned the trade of cabinet-maker, and afterwards carpenter trade; received good education in public schools of the city; enlisted in Twenty-seventh Missouri infantry; was sick at Sedalia, Mo., during siege of Lexington; returned to Wapello county and enlisted again, this time in Company E,

Twenty-second Iowa infantry; at siege of Vicksburg was severely wounded in the leg, rendering amputation necessary, laid for three months in the Lawson Hospital of St. Louis, receiving his final discharge before leaving there, in 1863. In 1864 he was elected county clerk, a position which he held for seven consecutive terms; was appointed revenue agent in 1883, and the following year appointed deputy collector; is a member of Cloutman Post, No. 69, G. A. R., also a member of the local I. O. O. F. lodge which he has represented in the Grand Lodge conclaves on several occasions; is a member of the Methodist church; is a republican, and has been since 1860.

B. H. FRENCH, Attorney-at-Law, 120 S. Court street, has been practicing law in Ottumwa for the past three years only, but by his untiring energy and close application to business he has built up one of the best law and collection businesses in the entire city. He is but thirty-five years of age, which gives him a great advantage in his efforts to build up a still greater clientage before he is compelled by old age to quit business life. He is entirely a self-made man, having started in life a poor boy, working his way up to where he now stands. He spent his early manhood in teaching school and pursuing his law studies, which made his task a difficult one; but he is at last reaping the fruits of his long struggle, having a splendid and rapidly increasing law practice. Aside from being an able lawyer he is a classical scholar, having graduated from two leading colleges. He is a close student and each day finds something added to his store of knowledge. Being a man of much force of character and determination, he rarely ever fails to succeed in anything he undertakes. Fidelity to a client's interests is one of the admirable traits of character possessed by him. Honest in purpose, he never involves his clients in unnecessary litigation and can always be relied upon to give an unprejudiced opinion as to their chances of success, though it lose him a good-sized fee.

3. B. H. French.

Ottumwa 1890

MANHATTAN SHOE HOUSE. Foland & Co., Retail Dealers in Fine Boots and Shoes, is one of the best known firms in the United States engaged in this line of business. Their main stores are located in New York City on Sixth and Eighth avenues, and are familiar to all devotees of fashion in the great metropolis. They carry an immense stock of all grades of goods, but give special attention to their trade in fine footwear for ladies and gentlemen. They keep constantly in stock a full line of the world-renowned J. and T. Cousins' shoes, and of which they make a decided specialty. The Cousins shoes are the finest, best wearing and most stylish shoes manufactured in this or a foreign country. In gentlemen's footwear of the finer grades they carry large stocks from the factories of such well known firms as Strong & Carroll, Johnston & Murphy, Hathaway, Soule and Harrington, and many others. Their sales of fine foot-wear will foot up more than the sales of all other stores combined, giving  evidence of the fact that the people of Ottumwa and the surrounding country are fully alive to the fact that for the best, most stylish and serviceable foot-wear they must patronize the Manhattan shoe store. The farmers of the country adjoining the city have learned that no other house carries boots and shoes suitable to their business equal in quality and workmanship to this firm's goods, the result of which is the bulk of the farmers' trade for Foland & Co. Mr. Edward Foland is the resident member of the firm, and a more pleasant, affable gentleman it would be difficult to find.

DR. J. E. WILKINSON, 120 Court street, Physician and Surgeon. Dr. Wilkinson came here from Missouri in 1875. The Doctor enjoys the distinction of being acknowledged one of the ablest physicians and surgeons in this part of the country, and of having one of the most extensive and lucrative practices. He graduated from the London Medical College, London, Eng., in 1859, and immediately started for America, landing with thirty-five cents in his pocket and among entire strangers. Pluck and energy, characteristic family traits, won, and to-day Dr. Wilkinson is one of the wealthiest and best-known physicians in the state. He is a member of the Wapello County Medical Society, permanent member of the American Medical Association and the Des Moines Valley Medical Association.

ADVERTISEMENT.

—THE—

CHICAGO, ROCK ISLAND AND PACIFIC

Is the Favorite Railway because it guarantees to the Traveling Public

Quick Time and Best Accommodations

At Uniformly Low Rates

From Chicago to all points West, Northwest and Southwest, and in correspondingly opposite directions.

Fast Solid Vestibuled Express Trains

With Through Service of Strictly First-class Day Coaches, Pullman Sleepers, Dining Cars and FREE Reclining Chair Cars between Chicago and Davenport, Des Moines, Council Bluffs and Omaha, and between Chicago and Denver, Colorado Springs and Pueblo via St. Joseph or via Kansas City and Topeka.

These trains are impenetrable to dust, well ventilated, and warmed by steam from the locomotive, having all the modern improvements that conduce to safety, comfort, and luxury.

FAST EXPRESS TRAINS

[Daily] from St. Joseph and Kansas City to and from all important Towns, Cities and Sections in Southern Nebraska, Kansas, Colorado, and Kingfisher, El Reno and Minco in the Indian Territory. Also via ALBERT LEA ROUTE to and from Watertown, Sioux Falls, Minneapolis and St. Paul, connecting for all points North and Northwest.

THE DIRECT AND POPULAR LINE

To Pike's Peak, Manitou, Garden of the Gods, Ute Park, Green Mt. Falls, Cascade, Glenwood Springs, and all other Sanitary and Scenic Resorts, and Hunting and Fishing Grounds of Colorado,—affording a choice of routes via Denver to or from Salt Lake City, Ogden, Helena, Butte, Portland (Ore.), Los Angeles and San Francisco.

For Tickets, Maps, Folders, or further information, apply to any ROCK ISLAND representative or Ticket Agent, or address at Chicago.

E. ST. JOHN,
General Manager.

JOHN SEBASTIAN,
Gen'l Ticket and Passenger Agent.

Ottumwa 1890

C. A. WALSH, of the law firm of Steck & Walsh, is a native of Iowa and one of the ablest young attorneys in the West. He has just been elected to the office of county attorney, sharing in the overwhelming victory of his party in Wapello county this fall. Mr. Walsh has been filling this position for the former county attorney, Mr. A. C. Steck, his partner, whose connection as counsel for the Colorado Iron & Coal Co. has kept him away for the past few months. Mr. Walsh was court reporter for nine years and was admitted to the bar in 1880. As a private citizen he occupies an enviable position, respected and admired by all, a man of strict integrity, a ripe scholar and a polished gentleman.

A. D. MOSS is one of the leading dry goods merchants of the city. As a business man he is acknowledged to be one of the shrewdest and best in the state. He has been in business here for over a quarter of a century, and during that time he has never for a moment forfeited the respect and confidence of the people.

A.D. Moss home - 507 W. Fourth

W. H. C. JAQUES, Attorney-at-law and Notary Public, is one of Ottumwa's leading lawyers and one of her most honored and highly respected citizens. He enjoys the reputation of being one of Iowa's ablest lawyers, taking rank with such men as Judge Burton, with whom he was formerly in partnership, and others. He was born in Washington county, Va., in 1841, moving with his parents to Fairfield, Iowa, in 1848, where he lived until 1867, when he removed to Ottumwa. He attended the Harvard Law school where he took a thorough legal course. Since beginning the practice of his profession he has enjoyed a clientage second to none in the city. A thorough gentleman and ripe scholar, he is a shining light in whatever company circumstances places him. In 1862 he enlisted as a private in Company D, Nineteenth Iowa Volunteer Infantry. In March, 1864, he was promoted to First Lieutenant of Company D, Fifty-sixth United States Colored Regiment and to the captaincy of the company in the fall of the same year. He was mustered out in 1866.

6. W. H. C. Jaques.

COL. S. A. FLAGLER is one of the liberal citizens of the town who always take a leading part in public enterprises. In Ottumwa he is one of a small band of leaders to whom the city is indebted for very much of its material progress and its reputation as an enterprising manufacturing town. In 1871 he was elected mayor of Ottumwa and served one term, declining a renomination on account of his many other duties. He is a member of the I. O. O. F., and has held all the different offices of the order. He is also a member of the Patriarchal Circle and is Supreme Oracle. Is vice-president of the Coal Palace Association, and a member of two of its committees.

Ottumwa 1890

W. S. CRIPS & BRO., 113 and 115 East Third street, Livery, Sale and Transfer Stables. This is the leading livery, feed and sales stable in the city, and the only transfer line. The proprietors, W. S. & S. P. Crips, are active, enterprising business men, who can always be relied upon, and who owe their splendid success to their efforts to please their patrons. Carriages for theaters, balls, weddings, etc., are always to be had on short notice. Their stables are clean and well ventilated, affording splendid accommodations for boarding. Both members of the firm are excellent judges of horse-flesh and make a specialty of buying and selling horses for others. Customers are always sure of courteous treatment, the best of rigs and low prices when they patronize Crips & Bro. They started business here in 1878. The bulk of the transportation business of this city is done by this firm, employing twelve two-horse drays and twenty-five hands. W. S. Crips is a member of the Knights of Pythias and the

Royal Arcanum. S. P. is a member of the Modern Woodmen of America Society and also of the Royal Arcanum. In connection with their large livery and transfer business they conduct one of the best equipped undertaking establishments in Iowa. This branch of their business is conducted in a separate building from the stables, occupying a large brick block, three stories high, all of which is devoted to this important department. No finer or larger stock of coffins and caskets can be found west of Chicago than is carried by this firm. Experienced in the handling, shipping and embalming of bodies, possessed of every possible facility for the prompt and rapid transaction of all orders, they guarantee satisfaction to all who transact business with them. A photograph of their beautiful funeral car, the finest and most expensive in the West, appears here.

THE OTTUMWA BUSINESS COLLEGE, one of the oldest and most successful in the state, have rented a floor in the new Y. M. C. A. building for a term of years. When completed their new location will afford them all the comforts of steam heat, electric light and sanitary conveniences. Their new commercial offices, including Merchants' Emporium, Commission, Real Estate, Insurance, etc., will be on the plan of Bryant & Stratton's offices in Chicago. The type-writing and short-hand departments will have separate rooms. Messrs. O'Brien & Gardner, the proprietors, have the unqualified endorsements of the citizens of the city and state, and they are both eminently qualified for their line of education.

Ottumwa 1890

J. F. DINGS, Grocer, 402 West Second street. Mr. Dings began business in his present quarters in January, 1889. He is one of the brightest, progressive and thoroughly enterprising men in the grocery business. He makes every effort possible to merit patronage and that he succeeds can be understood from the fact that he keeps four experienced salesmen constantly employed. He is a conscientious, straightforward business man, who has learned the art of attracting customers and of keeping them when once secured. His aim is to carry everything known to the trade in fine groceries, both domestic and foreign, and to sell them at prices that can not be lowered by competitors without a loss. Mr. Dings is one of those pleasing gentlemen who elevate their business to a higher standard by such honorable methods as are sure to meet with the universal approval of his patrons and the public. He is a man whom everybody respects and admires, and one whom the publishers of this book would give more extended mention if permitted, by him, to do so.

2. J. F. Dings.

VON HOLTZSCHUHERR & AYRES, Dealers in Drugs, Chemicals, Stationery and Surgical Instruments, Sundries, etc., are located at 116 East Main street, and are successors to Chambers & Co. This is one of the oldest as well as largest and finest drug stores in the city. They carry a very heavy stock of goods and do an immense annual business. They make a decided specialty of their prescription department, never using any but the freshest drugs of full quality strength in compounding a prescription. The members of the firm are Oscar von Holtzschuherr and Sylvester E. Ayres. Mr. Von Holtzschuherr has been in the drug business sixteen years, the last ten of which he owned the Central drug store in Creston, Iowa, which he sold in 1889. He spent a year in Europe, returning here in February, 1890. Mr. Ayres was formerly engaged in the drug business in Creston, Iowa, but for the past eleven years has been city ticket agent for the C. B. & Q. R. R. Both gentlemen are very popular and highly respected, and number many of the leading citizens of the city and state among their friends.

J. M. RANSIER, Livery and Undertaking establishment, 222, 224 East Second street. Mr. Ransier needs no introduction to the people of Ottumwa and surrounding towns, as he has lived and been in business here the greater portion of his life. In his livery stable he keeps the very best turnouts, and in his undertaking rooms the finest coffins, shrouds, etc. His funeral car is the finest in the state. His is the oldest livery and undertaking business in the city. He is an old soldier and an active member of the G. A. R., enlisting in the army when but sixteen years old. Mr. Ransier occupies his own building, a two-story and basement structure, which is especially adapted to the conduct of his business. Aside from this large establishment he owns and conducts one of the fittest and most extensive floral gardens in the state. For floral designs for wedding parties and funerals he excels all other florists. his aim is to cultivate every flower and plant possible to grow in this climate, however rare and delicate.

J. SEYMOUR, Cooperage and Box-Factory, Union street, on C. R. I. & P. R. R., one of the leading manufacturing establishments of the city, producing barrels, tubs, firkins, boxes, etc. The business was established by Mr. Seymour in 1877. His trade is greatest in southern Iowa and northern Missouri, but reaches points in Minnesota and Illinois. He employs thirty-five experienced hands and keeps two traveling salesmen on the road.

DR. J. W. CAMPBELL, Optician, 114 South Court street. Dr. Campbell is one of the most successful opticians in the country. He keeps a large stock of spectacles of domestic and foreign manufacture and is able to fit and strengthen the eyesight of all who require glasses, no matter what the affliction of the eyes. He is medical examiner for the C. B. & Q. Railroad and also U. S. Expert Pension examiner.

Ottumwa 1890

JOHN MORRELL & Co., Limited, Pork Packers, Lard Refiners and Jobbers. This large concern is a branch of the well-known English packing firm of John Morrell & Co., one of the largest in the world, and which was established in 1820. The branch here was opened in 1877 and the first building erected in 1878, since which time numerous additions have been made and still another, the largest of all, is now in process of construction and which will make of this one of the largest packing establishments in the United States. The company employs on an average of three hundred and fifty experienced men, a number that will be largely increased when the addition now being constructed is completed. The entire plant is to be lighted by electricity as soon as the new wing or addition is completed, thus enabling the company to run a night and day force while a new plant of the very latest improved machinery will be added. This is by great odds the largest concern in Ottumwa, and too much can not be said in praise of it and the benefits derived from its operation. It advertises Ottumwa in a manner not equalled by all the

John Morrell & Co. packing plant

T. D. Foster

other factories and mills of the city combined. Its products go to all states and territories west to the Rocky Mountains and south to the Gulf of Mexico. Seventy per cent. of the entire output goes to Europe, going as far north as the Russian frontier and south to Australia. The products of this firm's packing houses, and more especially those sent out from the branch house here, are of a superior quality and are possessed of a flavor that is relished by the lords and ladies of royal blood quite as keenly as it is by the humble country peasant. Whether this is due to the superiority of Iowa beeves and porkers or to some process of refining and packing known only to Morrell & Co. is a secret, but certain it is that their meats and lard are eagerly sought for and purchased in preference to all others. Mr. Thomas D. Foster, managing director of this large concern, and a resident here, has been in full control of it since its inception in 1877, and it is to his superior business ability and sagacity that its great success and marvelous growth are due. Mr. Foster is deeply interested in the growth and prosperity of Ottumwa, and is always foremost in advocating and assisting any and all enterprises that tend toward its advancement and improvement. Mr. Foster is a native of England but has spent most of his life in the United States, and is as patriotic an American as though he were the direct descendant of one of the Mayflower's passengers.

MCNETT & TISDALE, Attorneys-at-law, East Main street. This well-known law firm was organized in 1882. They practice in all the courts and do a general law business. Wm. McNett has practiced law since 1869, and W. D. Tisdale since 1878.

Ottumwa 1890

HARDSOCG'S DRILL FACTORY, Martin Hardsocg, owner and proprietor, foot of Vine street. The drill and machine shops of Mr. Hardsoeg are the largest of their kind, not only in the United States but in the world. The history of this great concern, and its able proprietor, reads like romance. Ten years ago Mr. Hardsocg was an humble, obscure resident of a little coal mining town west of Ottumwa, called Avery; to-day he is at the head of the largest factory, engaged in the manufacture of drills and coal mining machinery in the world, he is a self-made man. He began the manufacture of coal mining drills in a little country blacksmith shop. His drills were such a wonderful improvement over the old style that a demand was natural and instantaneous. With the drill of former years a miner would whack and scrape for from one to three hours to reach the depth desired for a shot, and when finished would leave the poor fellow in an exhausted condition. With the drill made by Mr. Hardsocg, having a post and gearing, the miner can drill a perfect hole in a very few moments, and without one-tenth the exhaustion resulting from the old method. The vast difference between the two methods can only be appreciated by the hard-working miner. The demand for these drills has increased so rapidly that it has been found necessary to increase the facilities to such an extent that to-day we find a factory one hundred feet square and three stories in height, employing about fifty skilled mechanics operating automatic machines for turning out these goods.

Since the establishment of this great concern here in 1880 the fame of its products have reached to the mining regions of this country and Europe. Orders from all parts of the world are continually coming in, and in increasing numbers. Four traveling salesmen are on the road, in the interests of the house, visiting all parts of the United States. The capacity of the factory will be doubled at once, and the working force increased accordingly. Aside from these famous drills the factory turns out a full line of miners' tools, and machinery of all kinds, including picks, wedges, sledges, tampers, scrapers, iron and copper needles, steel body cars, trucks, car-wheels, etc.

A word about Mr. Hardsocg will end this short sketch. He is a man of marked ability, and equally marked strength of character, a man of enterprise and energy, honorable and upright in all his dealings, honored and respected by all who know him.

The demand in the South and East made it necessary to establish a branch house at Charleston, W. Va.; the trade handled from this point is looked after by two traveling salesmen.

Ottumwa 1890

IOWA NATIONAL BANK 205 East Main street. This is one of the most conservative, and at the same time solid and substantial, of all the great financial institutions of the state. The bank was organized and opened in 1870 by Chas. F. Blake, James L. Taylor and several well known residents of Mt. Pleasant, Iowa. Mr. Blake has been the president of the bank since its organization with the exception of the three first years of its life, and its active and able manager. It is safe to say that no banker in Iowa is held in higher esteem, nor any who command the entire confidence of other bankers to the extent that Mr. Blake does. He is the embodiment of strict and rigid integrity in all his dealings, both public and private. He was born in Prussia in 1823, coming to this country in 1836 and to Ottumwa in 1845. He was formerly a resident of Hamilton county, Ohio, and of Indianapolis, Ind. In 1865 he engaged in the drug business, which he followed for nine years, the firm name being Taylor, Blake & Co. Always foremost in contributing to every public enterprise, he has become interested in nearly every large concern that has come to Ottumwa in the last twenty years. He has served the city as assessor, alderman, city treasurer, etc., for many years in succession, positions that have always come to him without solicitation. The bank has a capital stock of $100,000 and an undivided surplus of $50,000. Its officers are: Chas. F. Blake, president ; Wm. Daggett, vice-president; T. H. Eaton, cashier; and C. K. Blake, assistant cashier. Mr. C. K. Blake is the eldest son of Chas. F. Blake and one of the brightest and most promising young men engaged in the banking business.

1. C. K. Blake.

M. B. ROOT & SON, Marble and Granite, Cut-Stone and Building Material, 225 West Main street. This is one of the oldest, as well as the largest, concerns of the kind in the State of Iowa, and at the same time most reliable and satisfactory with which to do business. M. B. Root established the factory and yards in 1860, which he conducted alone until 1863, when, by the admission of a silent partner, he changed the name to Root & Co., under which title the business was done until 1880, when it was again changed to M. B. Root & Son, by the admission to full partnership of Frank L. Root, his son. While the firm name still remains M. B. Root & Son, the management and control of the business is entirely in the hands of the son, Frank L., his father having died a few months ago. Mr. Root is one of the brightest, enterprising and active young business men in Ottumwa, whose honorable, straight-forward methods are winning for him many friends and increased patronge [sic]. He employs eight thoroughly experienced men, and keeps two salesmen on the road continuously. His goods find a market all over Iowa, Missouri and Nebraska. In the cemetery in this city are to be found some excellent specimens of the beautiful work he does in the form of monuments over the graves of Mr. Leighton, Mr. Loomis and Mr. Taylor. He makes a specialty of fine monuments made from the famous Quincy and Barre granites, and from the still more famous, dark, variegated Columbian marble. Estimates are promptly furnished upon application on any class of work known to the trade. A very large stock of Louisville cement, Hannibal lime and plaster of paris are constantly kept on hand at the very lowest cash prices.

Ottumwa 1890

THE OTTUMWA MEDICAL AND SURGICAL INSTITUTE is one of the city's oldest and greatest advertising cards. It was founded eighteen years ago by Dr. J. Jackson Crider, a physician whose skill in the treatment of chronic and surgical diseases in both sexes has made him one of the most famous men of the present age. The people who have been restored to health and happiness at this infirmary can be found in all the middle and western states and territories—their names are registered and will be given to people who wish proof of the Doctor's skill before placing themselves under his treatment. In the treatment of catarrh, throat, lung, kidney, stomach, cancerous and female diseases of all kinds, he has repeatedly proven himself the complete master, bringing instant relief and rapid recovery, which never fails to prove permanent if his instructions are followed. His Infirmary is a large, commodious residence and located in the residence portion of the city. While especially fitted up for the treatment and cure of patients, it yet possesses all the comforts and conveniences of a home free from annoyance and restraint. The first year's

3. J. Jackson Crider, M. D.

business done by the Doctor after opening this place showed receipts aggregating $9,000. In 1875—76 the receipts were less on account of the financial distress occasioned by the immense rain-fall—one wet season following the other. For the last twelve years his receipts have averaged $15,000 each year, and yet he finds himself unable to show a balance on the right side of the ledger on account of the great cost of the medicines he uses, improvements and new and expensive instruments. The Doctor is not of that class who advertise "no cure, no pay;" he never takes a case until after a careful diagnosis he is confident of a cure and can guarantee complete recovery. He makes catarrh a specialty of his extensive practice. While in South America he discovered a specific remedy for catarrh, by means of which he can seat you in a chair, place a towel around your neck and a bowl in your lap, and in ten minutes will extract from one-half pint to a pint of mucus from your head and throat. If he fails he will give you $100. He will likewise pay $100 to any man or woman on earth who will do the same. In the Infirmary he employs two special physicians and a matron, who has charge of the nurses. From those suffering with Catarrh and Bright's Disease, and who think they are incurable, the Doctor is especially anxious to hear, and to whom he will send the names and addresses of the people who were afflicted with these dread diseases before placing themselves under his care and treatment.

Walter Tierney

J.H. Hammond

TIERNEY & HAMMOND, Tailors and Gents' Furnishing Goods, located in the Opera-House Block, is considered one of the best places in the city by devotees of fashion in which to secure the best goods for the least money, and all the latest styles and patterns. They do not confine themselves to the local trade, having two traveling salesmen on the road continuously. Some idea of the business conducted by them may be gained from the fact that they sold 10,000 pairs of pants last year, a figure that they promise to largely exceed in 1890. The firm is composed of W. E. Tierney and J. H. Hammond. Mr. Tierney is from Rockford, Ill., and is a thoroughly enterprising and energetic young business man of great promise and well liked by all who know him. Mr. Hammond has lived in Ottumwa for many years and is familiar to all society people of the city, among whom he is a great favorite. Like Mr. Tierney, he is a pushing, enterprising young man, whom everybody respects, and he is bound to make a leader in his chosen calling. The firm's wholesale trade reaches all towns in Iowa and Nebraska, and is rapidly extending to other states and territories.

Ottumwa 1890

ARTHUR GEPHART, Druggist, located at 206 East Main street, is one of the oldest and most popular merchants in the city. He, in company with Mr. Udell, established themselves in the drug business in their present location in 1879, which they conducted until 1881, at which time Mr. Udell retired, his interest being purchased by Mr. Gephart. A finer line of fresh drugs and drug-

4. Arthur Gephart.

gists' sundries, stationery, cigars, etc., can not be found in the State of Iowa. Mr. Gephart has a splendid patronage among the better class of people of Ottumwa. His prescription department is given special attention and is always under his direct supervision, although he employs a number of competent prescription clerks continuously. He makes a decided speciality of holiday goods during their season and carries one of the finest lines to be found in the city. He is a member of the Malta Commandery, No 31, Knight Templars, in which lodge he holds the position of E. C. He was born in Ottumwa in 1856, and has lived to see the city grow to its present metropolitan proportions.

Store of Arthur Gephart

The Ballingall Hotel - corner of E. Main and Green

THE BALLINGALL—Ottumwa's leading Hostelry, is to that great class of travelers and tourists who constitute so large a part of American society now-a-days, synonymous with Ottumwa, and is, without exaggeration, a model hotel. The Ballingall really merits extended space in dwelling upon the many features of metropolitan aspect in which this beautiful little city abounds. The opening of this hotel dates back as far as 1866, and its origin is due to its present owner, Mr. P. G. Ballingall, whose acquaintance and popularity among the hotel and traveling fraternities is not exceeded by any hotel man in the West. He was succeeded in 1882 by the present proprietor and landlord, Mr. J. C. Manchester, a gentleman ripe in experience in hotel management, who is making a most successful effort to merit the popularity and esteem enjoyed by his predecessor. How well he is succeeding is demonstrated by the fact that he has thoroughly established The Ballingall as the only first-class hotel in

Ottumwa 1890

Ottumwa; patronized only by the best and most exacting element of the ubiquitous world. Recent improvements have beautified the appearance, both the exterior and interior, and the weary traveler feels at once upon entering that he has reached an abode of comfort and luxury. The floors of the entire lower portion comprising the office, reading-room, wash-room, etc., etc., are laid with tiling, and the furnishings are of hard wood, elaborately carved and finished in natural colors. A fountain plays in the center of the spacious rotunda and a broad staircase leads both right and left to elegantly furnished corridors running around three sides of the office, resembling the balconies of the Sherman House in Chicago. Apart from this is a luxurious parlor the windows of which overlook the street. The dining-hall is a beautifully decorated room forty by sixty-five feet, in two sides of which are windows admitting an abundance of light. Set apart for the convenience of ladies and private parties are two ordinaries, 30x18 feet. The *Cuisine* is a specialty with this house. The following bill of fare was served on Sunday, September 7, 1890, and being no extraordinary event is a sample of the elegance of their dinner:

```
                              MENU.
   Consomme, aux Petits Pois                         Clam Chowder
                  Boiled Salmon Trout, Parsley Sauce
                   Fried White Fish, Saratoga Chips
                            Cream Slaw
   Leg of Mutton, French Capers
              Sugar Cured Ham, Wine Sauce
                                          Ox Tongue, Celery Sauce
   Sliced Cucumbers                                      Tomatoes
   Prime Ribs of Beef, Brown Gravy
             Loin of Pork, Baked Apples
                      Lamb, Mint Sauce
                           Young Turkey, Stuffed, Currant Jelly
   Fried Spring Chicken
              Escaloped Oysters
                   Sweetbreads, Breaded, French Peas
                            Peach Cobbler, Sauce Benedictine
   Celery                                             Shrimp Salad
   Summer Squash       Boiled or Mashed Potatoes      String Beans
       Baked Sweet Potatoes     Sugar Beets    Egg Plant Fried in Batter
   Apricot Pie                                     Cream Lemon Pie
                   Fruit Pudding, Brandy Sauce
          Vanilla Ice Cream                         Pear Meringue
   Assorted Cake                                       Mixed Nuts
         Water melon              Fruit                  Cheese
            Tea                   Coffee                  Milk
```

Main desk and lobby of the Ballingall

An especially pleasing feature of the Sunday dinners is the performance of a select programme of music by Professor Schwabkey's famous orchestra. The master of ceremonies in this department is Mr. R. M. Seeley, formerly of Chicago, who enjoys the reputation of being the finest head waiter in the State. He has had a life-long experience in the largest hotels of the country, is a popular favorite with everyone, and surprisingly alert to the wants of his guests. Socially he stands high and is one of the few thoroughly temperate and reliable men of his profession. The day clerk, Mr. Z. A. Frazier, a brother-in-law of Mr. Manchester, has had several years of hotel experience, is an old commercial man, and decidedly popular with the traveling fraternity. He came here from Vermont in 1888. Mr. J. W. Dayton, the night clerk, is an old experienced office man, having spent many years behind the "desk." He is a graduate of Washington University, St. Louis, and was a clerk in the Planter's House when it was

Ottumwa 1890

R.M. Seeley

the leading hotel of St. Louis. He has had some newspaper experience, having had charge of the circulation of the *Minneapolis News*, which he left to be the press representative of an amusement enterprise. Having had varied experiences in business and placed in positions to meet and judge of all kinds and sorts of men, he is admirably fitted for his present position. The tidy appearance of all parts of the house and the perfect attention that the rooms receive is due to the vigilance and care of the housekeepers, Mrs. J. O. Manchester and Mrs. Z. A. Frazier. They have a corps of most competent chamber maids, and keep the one hundred and thirty rooms which the hotel contains in excellent order. The entire working force of the house numbers thirty-five hands. There are two sample rooms on the first floor, and a drive way into the office. The house is heated entirely by steam and illuminated by gas and one hundred and fifty incandescent and seven arc lights. The cigar and news stand is conducted entirely by lady clerks. Mr. Manchester is a native of Connecticut, but came to Ottumwa from Muscatine, Iowa, where he resided for three years. A more quiet and unassuming gentleman is rarely found, and he has surrounded himself with willing hands and admiring friends by his kind and considerate treatment of all. He is one of Ottumwa's leading spirits and is enterprising in all things conducive to the city's advancement. He was captain of Syracuse Division, No. 3, Uniform rank, Second Regiment, Knights of Pythias, of this city for three years, and was elected Lieut. Colonel of this commandery, October 1, 1890. He is also a member of the Royal Arcanum, and has been an Odd Fellow for twenty years.

2011 edition

OTTUMWA MINERAL SPRINGS. Among the natural advantages and beautiful spots in which Ottumwa abounds, the citizens point with pride to the mineral springs which form the basis of one of the most successful curative institutions in the United States. About a mile and a half from the center of town, accessible by the electric motor cars and well-paved roadways, is located the Infirmary, Sanitarium and Surgical Institute of E. J. Shelton & Co., enjoying a reputation that extends to every state and territory between the two oceans. The natural location of this great health resort is one of its chief charms and advantages, and no visitor can possibly complete his detour of the city's beauties without a visit to this pleasant home for invalids. The opening of the springs happened to be in a deep ravine surrounded on all sides by green-clad hills—a cool and refreshing retreat in summer and a protection from the chilly winds of winter months. It was on this spot that L. E. Gray built and opened in 1883 the home-like sanitarium illustrated elsewhere. He was shortly afterwards succeeded by the present company, which is comprised of the

Ottumwa 1890

1. Dr. E. J. Shelton.

2. Dr. E. K. Shelton.

following well-known gentlemen: E. J. Shelton, M. D.; E. D. Beaucamp; E. K. and A. H. Shelton, all of whom are conspicuous for their skill and experience as successful physicians and surgeons. Each member of this Medical Board of Directors enjoyed a reputation not confined to Iowa or tributary states long before they associated themselves in the great work they have undertaken. The marvelous cures effected at this sanitarium testify to the truth of the statements contained in this article. To the afflicted, who have sought in vain for relief, and who may read this article, a ray of hope must come like a beam of bright sunshine breaking through the black clouds which crowd 'round the valley of despair and death. It will gladden their hearts when they read of what this noble band of men have done for suffering humanity; hope will give place to belief, and belief to conviction, as the records of wonderful surgical operations and successful cures are disclosed and proven by living witnesses.

Dr. E. J. Shelton has been United States pension examiner since 1865. For the removal of tumors of the abdomen and the treatment of diseases of women he has no equal in the West. He has had over forty years' experience as a physician and surgeon. The arrangement of the infirmary, so as to give every possible convenience and comfort to its guests, is perfect, including all modern improvements and excellent cuisine. The baths, to which thousands of restored invalids owe their life and health, are spacious and luxurious, including hot, cold and vapor baths, attended by skilled assistants well drilled in the various forms of the invigorating massage treatment. The water stands favorably and in some cases superior in comparison with the famous health-giving springs of the world. Comparisons are challenged in the following analysis from spring No. 1:

```
                    ANALYSIS OF
         ONE U. S. GALLON OF WATER (231 Cubic Inches).
                Spring No. 1, 314 feet deep.
Chloride Sodium ..................................... 51.805
Sulphate of Lime..................................... 38.230
Sulphate of Potassium................................  2.231
Sulphate of Sodium...................................200.875
Carbonate of Lime.................................... 22.265
Carbonate of Magnesium............................... 30.802
Carbonate of Iron....................................  2.940
Silicic Acid.........................................  7.299
Alumna ..............................................  trace
Organic Matter.......................................  trace
                                                      _____
     Total grains...................................855.447
     Also, free and half combined carbonic acid gas.
                                    J. D. CARTER,
                      Analytical Chemist Omaha Medical College.
```

It will be seen from the above that this water is the most physiological in combination, the strongest alkaline-saline waters ever discovered; a more perfect combination not to be found in any other mineral water. This water is shipped in any quantity to all parts of the world. It is unequalled as a table water, even more refreshing than Seltzer, and besides being a liver stimulant is a perfect laxative. Write to them for information relative to treatment, cures, prices, medicinal properties of the water, etc. The number of successfully cured cases that are discharged daily from this institution is surprising.

Ottumwa 1890

C. SAX & SON, Wholesale and Retail Dealers in Clothing and Merchant Tailoring, are in premises located at 233 and 235 East Main street. They are the acknowledged leaders in their business in Ottumwa, if not in the state; and carry a stock three times the size of that carried by any similar institution located here. The name of Sax & Son, upon any article of clothing, is a guaranty of "Superiority in quality" of goods, and also in workmanship and finish. This is one of the oldest, and at the same time most reliable firms in the city, having been in business here since 1861. The firm name until 1888 was C. Sax & Bro., at which time it was changed to C. Sax & Son, by the retirement of Mr Sax's brother, and the admission of his son Sidney J. Sax. They employ eight salesmen and fifteen tailors. The handsome business and office building they occupy was erected by them in 1883. Built of the most substantial materials and fitted up with all modern improvements, such as elevator, steam heat, electric lights, and the show-windows of French plate, among the largest in the city.

View from the Coal Palace tower looking southeast down Main Street

2011 edition

BUSINESS DIRECTORY.

Anderson & Co., A. P., Grocer, 106 East Main.
Anderson, J. P., Tailor, 330 East Main.
Amelang, Paul, Cigar Mfr., 133 West Main.
Armstrong, A. J., Paints, Oils, 105 North Market.
Adler, P. E., Ins., Real Estate, Loans, 212 East Main.
Atlantic Grocery, 636 West Main.
Ainley, J., Flour Mills, South Side.
Almeyer & Son, B., Clothing, 209 East Main.
Biddison, P. C., Hardware, 123 East Main.
Briggs & Emery, Lawyers, 120 Court street.
Baker L. J., Physician, 226 East Main.
Boltz, T. J., Lawyer, cor. Court and Second.
Bickley, J. R., Justice, 109 South Market.
Black Diamond Coal Co., Summers Building.
Ball & Myers, Real Estate, cor. Court and Second.
Bishop, II. E., Telephone Co., West Main street.
Bowles, J. T., Job Printer, 114 East Main.
Briggs, Mrs. L. T., Milliner, 208 East Main.
Burton, S. H., County Surveyor, 111 South Market.
Bingham, C., Cigar Mfr., 125 East Second.
Berry Bros., Dry Goods, South Side.
Bothwell, J. W., Grocer, South Side.
Baker Bros., Butter and Eggs, 220 College.
Burgess, J. R., Farm Machinery, 112 Market.
Cockerill, H. M., Teas, Coffees, cor. Second and Market.
Chicago Shoe Store, A. Hayward, 211 East Main.
Christie, W. S., Real Estate, Insurance, Loans, 106 East Main.
City Savings Bank, 115 South Market.
Cascade Laundry, 406 East Main, A. Westling, Prop.
Corey, W. W., Lawyer, East Main.
Coen & Siberell, Lawyers, 121 East Main.
Chilton, Jacob, Contractor and Builder, 1308 North Court.
Curran & Kelly, Ice Dealers, Mechanic street.

Ottumwa 1890

Commercial Hotel, cor. 4th and Washington.
Criley & Leonard, Insurance, Real Estate, 132 East Main.
Cooper & Son, Furniture, 127 Main.
Douglas, T. J., Physician, 207 South Green street.
Depot Hotel, Stephen Long, Manager.
Dutro, H. L., Grocer, 456 North Jefferson street.
Davis & Miller, Grocers, 903 West Second.
Dawson, Z. T., Grocer, 132 East Main.
Dungan & Culbertson, Grocers, 128 East Main.
Devol, A. B., Livery, cor. Court and Third streets.
Dutro, L. H , Grocer, 103 South Market.
Detrich & Capell, Sash, Doors, Blinds, 314 West Main.
Dingee Pickle Co., O. S, Old Packing House.
Davis, A. A., Physician, 112 Court.
Edgerly & Co., J. W., Wholesale Druggists, Market and Third.
Eldon Coal and Mining Co., 109 South Market.
Eaton, Daniel, Furniture Factory, 325 Samantha.
Emery, D. H., Lawyer, 105 East Main.
Fields, W. G., Newsdealer, Market and Second.
Fischer, John C., Capitalist, 132 West Fifth.
First National Bank, W. B. Bonnifield, Pres., Main street.
Field, R. S., Jeweler, 117 East Main.
Ferbers Fair, Dry Goods, etc., 112 Main.
Ford, C. E,, Livery, 111 West Second.
Fair & Williams, Bridge Works, 403 South Vine.
Fry, Joseph, Grocer, South Side.
French, B. H., Lawyer, 120 Court street.
Frey, J. A., Dentist, 120 Court street.
Graves, Geo. H., Grocer, 103 North Court.
Golden Eagle Clothing Store, 229 East Main.
Grube, F. W., Gents' Furnishings, 226 East Main.
Globe Tea Co., 216 East Main.
Galey, W. M., Insurance, Real Estate, Court and Second.
Gray, J. W., Grocer, 105 South Court.
Graves, A. L., Horticulturist, Second and Caldwell.
Gilchrist, R. S., Physician, 130 East Main.
Griswold, Geo., Lawyer, 105 North Court.
Harper, Chambers & Co., Hardware, 125 East Main.

2011 edition

Hinsey, J. C., Physician, 120 Court.
Healy, Thos., Hardware, 224 East Main.
Hammond & Moore, Loans, Insurance, 112 East Main.
Hahn Bros., Grocers, 835 East Main.
Hessen & Co , Decorators, Painters, 121 East Second.
Haw & Co, Geo., Hardware, cor. Second and Market.
Harned & Sullivan, Undertakers, 115 West Second.
Holmes, L. A., Confectioner, 831 South Green.
Hall, Chas.. Lawyer, 106 East Main.
Hyatt, B. F., Physician, 120 South Court.
Hawkins, W. H., Contractor, 809 West Fourth.
Harlan & Co., Druggists, 101 East Second.
Hughes, S. W., Upholsterer, 123 West Second.
Hissem & Nicklin, Dry Goods, 634 West Main.
Hall, T. J., Contractor, 305 West Ottumwa.
Jordan & Sons, W. A., Dry Goods, 230 Main.
Jones & Buchanan, Flour, Feed, 120 East Second.
Johnston & Van Der Veer, Grocers, McLane [sic] and Second.
Kister & Bayliss, Hardware, 118 East Main.
Kubitshek, M., Grocer, 311 East Main.
Kirk & Tisdale, Lumber, Third street.
Kilser & Pierson, Flouring Mills, Cass street.
Kendall & Bremhorst, Grocers, Court and Second.
Lac Lede Hotel, Eugene Talbot, Prop., Main street.
Lowenberg Bros., Bakery, 112 Court.
Loeb, Tobias, Cigar Factory, 304 East Main.
Loan and Building Association, J. D. Ferree, secretary, Court street.
Loomis, F. P. & Co., Jewelers, 120 East Main.
Lain, D. S., Confectioner, South Side.
Lockwood, J., Physician, 109 South Ash.
Lyman, O. W., Lawyer, 109 South Market.
Lewis, C. G., Physician, 116 South Green.
Lunkley, John, Restaurant, 208 South Market.
La Point, Mrs., Millinery, South Side.
Morey & Meyers, Cigar Mfrs., West Main.
Major & Co., C. W., Lumber, Washington and Second.
Mangan, J. M., Physician, 207 East Main.
Martin, Chas., Tailor, 207 East Main.

Ottumwa 1890

McDonald, W. F., Dentist, 107 North Court.
McCarroll & Son, Hardware, 105 East Main.
McKechnic, N., Physician, cor. Court and Second.
McCullough, S. C., Physician, 720 West Fourth.
Miller, D. F., Lawyer, 118 East Main.
Miller, J., Vet. Surgeon, 113 East Third.
McElroy, M. E. & Co., Grocers, cor. Jefferson and Grant.
Murphy, P. B., Murphy House, 1019 Sherman.
McCoy, H. N., Contractor, 125 Mill.
Michael & Sloan, Insurance, Real Estate, Room 7 Summers Building.
Mueller, H. F., Bakery, 223 West Main.
Merrill & Co., J. H., Wholesale Grocers, cor. Market and Third.
Meek, J. G., Dry Goods, 132 East Main.
Miller, C., Tinware Factory, 217 East Main.
Novelty Book Store. M. A. Dayton, 303 East Main.
National Starch Co., Wm. Daggett, Pres.
Nash, E. D., Photographer, 228 East Main.
O'Neil, S. E., Physican, 314 East Main.
Ottumwa Buggy Co., W. A. Carnes, Mgr., East Second.
Ottumwa Co-operative Coal Co., cor. Court and Second.
Orr, W. L., Justice cor. Market and Main.
Ottumwa Electric Ry., Market.
Ottumwa Linseed Oil Works, W. T. Harper, Mgr.
Ottumwa Savings Bank, cor Court and Main.
Ottumwa Screen Co., 106 South Marion.
Ottumwa National Bank, cor. Market and Main.
Ottumwa Blank Book and Pub. Co., 113 Main.
Ottumwa Cutlery Co., Foot Tisdale street.
Ottumwa Steam Laundry, 316 South Market.
Ottumwa Gas Co., East Samantha.
Ottumwa Box Factory, South Side.
Pickell, J. B., Grocer, 702 McLane [sic].
Prugh & Co., J., Crockery, 126 East Main.
Perdue, John F., Newsdealer, 223 East Main.
Platt & Hoyland, Milliners, 226 East Main.
Peterson, A. P., Grocer, 332 East Main.
Peters, H. C., Druggist, 101 Court.
Pickler & Schafer, Flour and Feed, 630 East Main.

2011 edition

Porter Bros. & Hackworth, Harness, etc., 104 East Main.
Pratt House, cor. Court and Second.
Roberts, H. W., Physician, 111 South Market.
Rankin, W. W., Lawyer, 105 North Court.
Riordan, T., Justice, 113 Market.
Reece, W. M., Contractor, Fourth.
Riordan, P. H., Lawyer, 201 Main.
Rogers, L. B. & Bro., Dyeing, 329 East Main.
Reifsnyder & Son, Chas., Fish and Meats, 516 East Main.
Rogers, L. E. & Bro., Dentists, Sax Bldg., Main.
Reynolds, G. W., Druggist, Main street and Iowa avenue.
Schworn, Adam, Grocer, 1564 East Main.
Sampson, J. W., Druggist, South Side.
Spragg & Son, Jas., Furniture, 211 South Market.
Smith, J. B., Hides, etc., 220 South Market.
Schilling, C. R., Boots and Shoes, 107 South Court.
Singer Sewing Machine Co., 115 East Main.
Stevens, O. C., Boots and Shoes, 115 Court.
Sutton, Lewis M., Painter, 111 South Mar1et.
Schwabkey, C. F., Musical Director, 113 East Second.
Smith, J. J., Lawyer, 128 East Main.
Spillman, S. A., Physician, 236 East Main.
Sisson, H. B., Physician, 133 Lincoln avenue.
Scott, B. W., Lawyer, 105 South Market.
Teeter, R. B., Contractor, 327 Sherman.
Thomas, F. M., Contractor, 107 West Main.
Tindell, N. M., Grocer, 108 South Market.
Van Sant, J. W., Music dealer, 115 East Main.
Van De Ven, H., Druggist, South Side.
Wilson, J. E., Druggist, 634 West Second.
Wagner, J. A., *Freie Presse*, 109 South Court.
Winter & Caster, Wagons, etc., 117 West Second.
Wing, John P., Butcher, 108 North Court.
Western Machine Works, 321 West Main.
Whitebreast Fuel Co., Market.
Waddington, W. M., Dry Goods, 113 South Court.
Work & Blake, Lawyers, Court and Second.
Whitaker, I. B., Physician, 427 West Second.

Ottumwa 1890

Westerhoff, B., Tailor, East Main.
Wertz, H. L., Jeweler, 827 Green.
Wagner Bros. & Slaven, Planing Mill, South Side.
Williamson, J., Physician, 107 North Court.
Williams, A. O., Physician, 120 Court.
Zambitzer, F. F., Box Factory, 211 East Main.
Zulauf, Henry, Woolen Mills, 223 South Jefferson.

ADVERTISEMENT.

OPERATING OVER

1000 MILES OF ROAD
IN IOWA, MINNESOTA AND DAKOTA.

SOLID TRAINS Between

CHICAGO, MINNEAPOLIS AND ST. PAUL
VIA THE FAMOUS ALBERT LEA ROUTE.
ST. LOUIS, MINNEAPOLIS AND ST. PAUL
VIA ST. LOUIS, MINNEAPOLIS & ST. PAUL SHORT LINE.

... AND ...

THROUGH SLEEPERS
.. BETWEEN ..
KANSAS CITY, MINNEAPOLIS & ST. PAUL,
ROCK ISLAND, CEDAR RAPIDS AND SIOUX FALLS, DAK.

CHICAGO AND CEDAR RAPIDS
VIA THE FAMOUS ALBERT LEA ROUTE.

· **THE SHORT LINE** ·
.. TO ..
——SPIRIT LAKE——
THE GREAT IOWA SUMMER RESORT.

For Railway and Hotel Rates, Descriptive Pamphlets and all information, address Gen'l Ticket and Pass. Ag

FOR CHEAP HOMES

On line of this road in Northwestern Iowa, Southeastern Minnesota and Central Dakota, where drought and crop failures are unknown. Thousands of choice acres of land yet unsold. Local Excursion rates given. For full information as to prices of land and rates of fare, address Gen'l Ticket and Passenger Agent.

Maps, Time Tables, Through Rates and all information furnished on application to Agents. Tickets on sale over this route at all prominent points in the Union, and by its Agents, to all parts of the United States and Canada.

☞ For announcements of Excursion Rates, and local matters of interest, please refer to the local columns of this paper.

C. J. IVES,   **J. E. HANNEGAN,**
Pres't & Gen'l Supt.   Gen'l Tkt. & Pass. Agt.

CEDAR RAPIDS, IOWA.

ADVERTISEMENT.

Chicago, Milwaukee & St. Paul Railway.

Electric Lighted and Steam Heated Vestibuled Trains, with Westinghouse Air Signals, between Chicago, St. Paul and Minneapolis, daily.

Through Parlor Cars on day trains between Chicago, St. Paul and Minneapolis.

Electric Lighted and Steam Heated Vestibuled Trains between Chicago, Council Bluffs and Omaha, daily.

Through Pullman Vestibuled Sleeping Cars, daily, between Chicago, Butte, Seattle, Tacoma, and Portland, Oregon.

Daily Trains, between St. Paul, Minneapolis and Kansas City via the Hedrick Route.

Through Pullman Sleeping Cars, daily, between St. Louis, St. Paul and Minneapolis.

Finest Dining Cars in the World.

The best Sleeping Cars. Electric Reading Lamps in Berths.

6,100 miles of road in Illinois, Wisconsin, Northern Michigan, Iowa, Minnesota, Missouri, South Dakota and North Dakota.

Everything First-Class.

First-Class People patronize First-Class Lines.

Ticket Agents everywhere sell Tickets over the Chicago, Milwaukee and St. Paul Railway.

For information address

GEO. H. HEAFFORD,
General Pass. and Ticket Agent,
Chicago, Ill.

For more information about these and other books, calendars and products, visit
www.pbllimited.com
PBL Limited
P.O. Box 935
Ottumwa Iowa 52501

  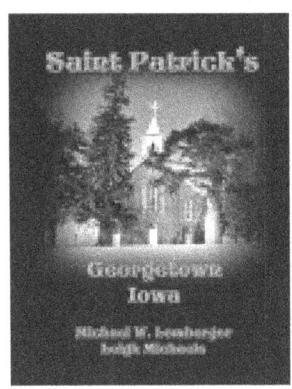 

www.ingramcontent.com/pod-product-compliance
Lightning Source LLC
Chambersburg PA
CBHW080249170426
43192CB00014BA/2620